"In creative ways Vickers juxtaposes Adam, Abraham, Israel, and the Mosaic law respectively with their supreme and crowning counterpart—Jesus, the obedient second Adam, the fulfillment of the promise to Abraham, and the atonement as the goal of the Mosaic law."
   —Hans F. Bayer, Covenant Theological Seminary

"Vickers has done the church a service, not by laboring through the recent challenges for a negative result, but by offering a positive, fresh exposition from the Scriptures. With breathtaking scope he traces Christ's imputed righteousness from the pages of Genesis all the way to Paul and James."
   —A. Andrew Das, Elmhurst College

"In the important debate about justification that continues within much contemporary evangelical theology and church life, Brian Vickers provides sound biblical and theological instruction on the key issues involved. With questions for guiding study and further reflection included, it will serve a broad audience: pastors and other church leaders, college and seminary students as well as their teachers, and others with an interest in these issues."
   —Richard B. Gaffin Jr., Westminster Theological Seminary

"Brian Vickers is both a brilliant scholar and a faithful teacher. In his new book, *Justification by Grace through Faith,* he offers both theological edification and spiritual encouragement. Those who love the gospel will welcome this new book."
   —R. Albert Mohler Jr., The Southern Baptist Theological Seminary

"Brian Vickers's *Justification* is a delightful read with its pastoral warmth and engaging style. Too easily and too often this crucial doctrine becomes merely an abstract, academic debate. Vickers, while aware of the debates, constantly roots the discussion in the impact and benefit this teaching should have for life according to the Scriptur⟨...⟩ ⟨...⟩ng this material in seminary and missions settings are apparent as he explains carefully and well, writing in a way that flows easily. I warmly commend it to all."

—**Ray Van Neste,** Union University

"This book is a positive, clear, constructive treatment of the biblical doctrine of justification by faith. Vickers is never unaware of the present-day narratives on this doctrine and he allows them to inform his discussion where necessary, but he does not stray from his purpose of letting the progressive biblical narrative determine the elements of his treatment. His personal conversation with Protestant confessional developments is ever present, giving consistency and historic substance to his discussion, but it does not override his relentless movement from the biblical text to doctrinal formation. The treatment is fulsome—Adam and Christ, Abraham and Christ, Moses and Christ, covenantal unity and personal responsibility, imputation and transformation, Paul and James, the Law, the cross, and the Spirit—and results in a high-quality presentation of a central biblical teaching. It is accessible in its diction, illustrations, and careful and clear development of paragraph-to-paragraph and chapter-to-chapter thought, but it finally allows entrance to those who are convinced that learning about justification is an important, perhaps supremely vital, pursuit for all people."

—**Tom J. Nettles,** The Southern Baptist Theological Seminary

"Vickers's new work is to be warmly welcomed. Here we find a clear and accessible and, most importantly, biblical restatement of what the Scriptures teach about justification."

—**Thomas R. Schreiner,** The Southern Baptist Theological Seminary

"Written discussions of justification are often topical or historical in bent, and understandably so. Brian Vickers has produced a concise and Reformed survey of justification that is exegetical and biblical-theological in focus. Taking us from Genesis to the

New Testament—and never losing us along the way—he admirably shows the flowering and unfolding of the doctrine of justification in Scripture. Vickers's scholarship makes this informed study an important contribution to the literature. Well-organized and accessibly written chapters and study questions, as well as a pastor's heart, make it a delight to read. I heartily commend it."
—**Guy Prentiss Waters,** Reformed Theological Seminary

"For nearly half a century now the historic and biblical doctrine of justification has been hotly debated. Brian Vickers lays hold of the wealth of wisdom produced by this debate, seen in the light of his years of study and rich international teaching experience. The result is a well-organized and gripping synthesis of the many biblical passages that speak to the simple but infinitely profound question posed by the Philippian jailer: "What must I do to be saved?" Vickers shows that the answer lies first of all in what God in Christ has done. It is hard to imagine a more wide-ranging, sure-footed, and user-friendly study upholding the doctrine by which, indeed, the true church stands or falls."
—**Robert W. Yarbrough,** Covenant Theological Seminary

Justification by Grace through Faith

Explorations in Biblical Theology

Anointed with the Spirit and Power: The Holy Spirit's
Empowering Presence
The Elder: Today's Ministry Rooted in All of Scripture
Election and Free Will: God's Gracious Choice and Our
Responsibility
Justification by Grace through Faith: Finding Freedom from
Legalism, Lawlessness, Pride, and Despair
Life Everlasting: The Unfolding Story of Heaven
The Nearness of God: His Presence with His People
Our Secure Salvation: Preservation and Apostasy
A Theology of James: Wisdom for God's People
A Theology of Mark: The Dynamic between Christology and
Authentic Discipleship
Wisdom Christology: How Jesus Becomes God's Wisdom for Us

Robert A. Peterson, series editor

Justification by Grace through Faith

Finding Freedom from Legalism, Lawlessness, Pride, and Despair

Brian Vickers

P&R
PUBLISHING
P.O. BOX 817 • PHILLIPSBURG • NEW JERSEY 08865-0817

ISBN: 978-1-59638-050-9 (pbk)
ISBN: 978-1-59638-571-9 (ePub)
ISBN: 978-1-59638-572-6 (Mobi)

Compass image © istockphoto.com

Printed in the United States of America

Library of Congress Cataloging-in-Publication Data

Vickers, Brian, 1966-
   Justification by grace through faith : finding freedom from legalism, lawlessness, pride, and despair / Brian Vickers.
       p. cm. -- (Explorations in biblical theology)
   Includes bibliographical references and indexes.
   ISBN 978-1-59638-050-9 (pbk.)
   1. Justification (Christian theology) 2. Grace (Theology) I. Title.
   BT764.3.V533 2012
   234'.7--dc23
                        2012026410

For Tom Schreiner,
Teacher, Colleague, Friend, Brother in Christ

Contents

Series Introduction

BELIEVERS TODAY need high-quality literature that attracts them to good theology and builds them up in their faith. Currently, readers may find several sets of lengthy—and rather technical—books on Reformed theology, as well as some that are helpful and semipopular. Explorations in Biblical Theology takes a more midrange approach, seeking to offer readers the substantial content of the more lengthy books, while striving for the readability of the semipopular books.

The series includes two types of books: (1) some treating biblical themes and (2) others treating the theology of specific biblical books. The volumes dealing with biblical themes seek to cover the whole range of Christian theology, from the doctrine of God to last things. Representative early offerings in the series focus on the empowering of the Holy Spirit, justification, the presence of God, and preservation and apostasy. Examples of works dealing with the theology of specific biblical books include volumes on the theology of the Psalms and Isaiah in the Old Testament, and books on the theology of Mark and James in the New Testament.

Explorations in Biblical Theology is written for college seniors, seminarians, pastors, and thoughtful lay readers. These volumes are intended to be accessible and not obscured by excessive references to Hebrew, Greek, or theological jargon.

Each book seeks to be solidly Reformed in orientation, because the writers love the Reformed faith. The various theological themes and biblical books are treated from the perspective of biblical theology. Writers either trace doctrines through the Bible or open up the theology of the specific books they treat.

Writers desire not merely to dispense the Bible's good information, but also to apply that information to real needs today.

Explorations in Biblical Theology is committed to being warm and winsome, with a focus on applying God's truth to life. Authors aim to treat those with whom they disagree as they themselves would want to be treated. The motives for the rejection of error are not to fight, hurt, or wound, but to protect, help, and heal. The authors of this series are godly, capable scholars with a commitment to Reformed theology and a burden to minister that theology clearly to God's people.

Robert A. Peterson
Series Editor

Foreword

DO WE REALLY NEED another book on justification? Haven't these issues been rehearsed over and over again? Is there anything new to say? Martin Luther rightly observed that we need to relearn the gospel every day, since we are so prone to forget it. What is true of individuals is also true of each generation. We don't learn about justification merely by studying what the Reformers or other venerable ancestors wrote on the subject. Such study, of course, is immensely valuable. Still, understanding justification is finally a spiritual matter. The Spirit of God helps us to comprehend the things of God (1 Cor. 2:12–13). This understanding is granted to us, as Luther taught us, in the midst of our trials, sufferings, and afflictions. We grasp the significance of justification the more we understand ourselves, the more we see deeply into our hearts, the more the Holy Spirit reveals to us our own selfishness and idolatry. And such self-comprehension is furnished through our sufferings.

The necessity of spiritual understanding explains why we can read formulations about justification that are accurate and still fail to comprehend the truth about our standing before God. Theologians prize precise formulations, and surely expressing and explaining the truth rightly is essential. Genuine understanding, however, must not be equated with grasping propositions, as if distinct and clear mental ideas were all that is needed. We need something deeper than (although not less than) mental cognition, which is why John Calvin begins the *Institutes* by saying that true theology stems from a knowledge of God and a knowledge of ourselves. A theologian isn't formed solely in the study but also in the crucible of life. In other words, we won't and can't learn about justification apart from the work of the Holy Spirit. Apprehending justification is a miracle of grace. It can never be reduced to a formula.

I love this book by Brian Vickers. I don't love it simply because he is a dear friend. I love it because it is the first book I would give to anyone interested in learning about justification. Let me explain why. First, Vickers sets justification in the context of the story line of the Bible. He doesn't just give us an abstract and sterile explanation of the doctrine. We learn how justification fits with the biblical story and how it fits with our story. What we find here is biblical theology at its best. Justification is explained in light of the whole canon of Scripture.

Second, the writing is engaging. I have read many books on justification, but I found this book hard to put down. It drew me in with its insights and ruminations on the doctrine. I think it drew me in because the book weaves together so well the exegetical, theological, and practical. Vickers says things in fresh ways, which helped me to grasp anew how stunning and wonderful justification is. I sensed in reading the book that the author knows his own heart and so he knows our hearts. Hence, he administers well the medicine of justification to troubled souls, to those who ache to know whether they are right with God.

Third, it may seem that I have left out a central truth. No one understands justification apart from the Spirit, but the Spirit illumines and casts light on the Word of God. Martin Luther was a professor of biblical exegesis for many years, and his intense study of Romans, Psalms, and other Scriptures was the means by which he came to understand the meaning of the righteousness of God. The Spirit doesn't work in a vacuum, for the Spirit helps us to interpret what is deposited in the Scriptures.

What characterizes this work by Vickers is a clear and convincing interpretation of the Scriptures. He sets forth in a compelling way what the Scriptures teach on justification, listening patiently to all that they teach on the matter and expounding it with clarity and conviction.

My prayer is that readers will be informed, challenged, encouraged, and comforted as they read, as they are reminded anew that our righteousness is not in ourselves but in Jesus Christ our Lord.

Thomas R. Schreiner
James Buchanan Harrison Professor of
New Testament Interpretation
The Southern Baptist Theological Seminary

Acknowledgments

I WANT TO OFFER a word of thanks to all the people who have helped me along the way of writing this book.

- Colleagues here at The Southern Baptist Theological Seminary who have either read parts of the book or discussed with me so many of the texts and issues related to justification: Gregg Allison, Jim Hamilton, Peter Gentry, Mark Seifrid, Tom Nettles, Bruce Ware, Steve Wellum, and Shawn Wright.
- A special word of thanks goes to Tom Schreiner for reading the entire manuscript and offering suggestions and insights.
- Jason McClanahan, pastor of Randolph Street Baptist Church, Charleston, West Virginia, for his encouragement to write a book for pastors and students and for reading over the manuscript during the last stages.
- Elijah Hixson, my assistant, for working on the index, checking sources, and reading over the manuscript.
- The students in my justification class for their careful work and thoughtfulness.
- Robert Peterson for his patience with me over the extended time it took to finish this book and for his care of the manuscript; to Robert's T.A. Elliott Pinegar for valuable editorial work; and to the editorial team at P&R, particularly John J. Hughes.
- The administration and trustees of The Southern Baptist Theological Seminary for granting a sabbatical to finish the book.

- David Simmons for his years of friendship and all his encouragement through the entire process of writing this book.
- Thom Smith, without whom I would not be where I am today.
- Finally, to my wife Denise, my partner in everything.

Introduction

"Look unto Me and Be Ye Saved"

ONE EVENING in the nineteenth century, a young C. H. Spurgeon visited a small church where a man was preaching from Isaiah 45:22: "Look unto me, and be ye saved, all the ends of the earth: for I am God, and there is none else." When Spurgeon left that church that evening, he was not the same man who had walked in earlier. His gaze, his heart, and his faith had been directed outside himself toward God. Here is his account of what he heard and experienced that night:

> He [the preacher] began, "'Look,' that is not hard work. You need not lift your hand, you do not want to lift your finger. Look, a fool can do that. It does not need a wise man to look. A child can do that. It don't need to be a full-grown to use your eyes. Look, a poor man may do that, no need of riches to look. Look, how simple; how simple." Then he went on, "'look unto me.' Do not look to yourselves, but 'look to me, that is Christ. . . . Look unto Jesus Christ;'" and then he went on in his own simple way to put it thus: "'Look unto me; I am sweating great drops of blood for you; look unto me, I am scourged and spit upon; I am nailed to the cross, I die, I am buried, I rise and ascend, I am pleading before the Father's throne, and all this is for you.'"[1]

1. C. H. Spurgeon, "Temple Glories," in *The Metropolitan Tabernacle Pulpit*, vol. 7 (Pasadena, TX: Pilgrim Publications, 1969, 1973), 224. The KJV is the translation most likely heard by Spurgeon.

1

Spurgeon was led away from himself and his own efforts, means, and works to Christ alone. He was converted, saved through faith in Christ. There are many ways to describe salvation through Christ, but no description is complete unless it stresses this one thing: that help and hope, forgiveness and righteousness, and freedom and assurance are found only by turning away from ourselves to believe in Christ's all-sufficient work.

In the context of the sermon text that C. H. Spurgeon heard that night (Isa. 45:22), God the Judge calls the people, hopelessly lost in idolatry (the heart of works righteousness), to stand before him and present their case. Of course, they have no case to make; their only plea is *guilty*. God is the Creator (v. 18) who reveals himself and who speaks "the truth" and proclaims "what is right" (v. 19), and their sole hope is in him, the only God and Savior (v. 21). He knows their sin, their idolatry, their hard-heartedness, but he does not tell them to try to do a better job, or to reform themselves, or to meet him halfway. God the merciful judge simply calls them to look to him. That is the background for the great gospel call: "Turn to me and be saved." That is the offer to everyone, to "all the ends of the earth." In New Testament terms, we might say to "both Jews and Gentiles." Salvation for everyone comes only one way: through faith in God.

Justification, foundational for salvation, is the legal declaration from God that a person stands before him forgiven and as one who lives up to the entirety of God's will. It absolutely depends on turning, by faith, away from our own works to receive God's verdict of "righteous" in Christ as a pure gift. In justification by faith in Christ alone, God speaks the truth and proclaims what is right in his eyes. Justification is not the whole of salvation or of the gospel, but it provides what is necessary to make us right with God and reorients us toward God's ultimate goal in creation and salvation of having a people who trust him and, as a result of that trust, obey him from the heart. The goal for which God created us is reached only through sinners' being justified, forgiven, and counted righteous in Christ—all by grace through faith. Justification by faith is not the whole of the gospel, but there is no gospel without justification by faith.

Justification: Not in Ourselves but in Christ Alone

Compare the perspective in Isaiah 45 to this statement: "We deplore efforts to denigrate human intelligence, to seek to explain the world in supernatural terms, and to look outside nature for salvation."[2] Consider that last clause again: "We deplore efforts . . . to look outside nature for salvation." I take it that "nature" includes not just the outside physical world but the nature within as well— the individual human being. As Christians, we read that and shake our heads at how entirely wrong and hopeless that statement really is. It should not, however, surprise us all that much that ordinary people, apart from the "supernatural" work of God, would say and believe such a thing. Too often we engage people as though we expect them to see things in ways we know on biblical grounds to be impossible apart from God's revelation. Of course, the lack of special revelation excuses no one; just the opposite is the case: the general revelation comprehended by all is enough to hold everyone accountable (see Rom. 1:18–23.). Nevertheless, what should concern us more than the fact that secular humanists want to rely on nothing outside themselves for salvation (whatever that means to them) is the shocking reality that people who call themselves *Christians* rely on practically everything for salvation except what lies outside themselves. It is one thing for secular humanists to trust in themselves; it is an altogether different matter for Christians who claim salvation in Christ alone to cling to self-reliance and self-justification.

Before our mental list of "those Christians" who do such things grows longer, we should turn the mirror around and say "we Christians." Inside each of us lurks the same tendency shared

2. The statement comes from Paul Kurtz, "The Affirmations of Humanism: A Statement of Principles," in *Free Inquiry* 25, 1 (December 2004/January 2005). The Statement of Principles may be purchased as no less than a "parchment copy . . . suitable for framing."

by our father Adam, namely, that in spite of knowing what God says, what he expects, and what he promises, we want to turn from him to ourselves and our own better plans. We do this in many ways, often cloaked in words, actions, and slogans that are all quite religious, orthodox, conservative, and pious—but we do it nonetheless. This is why we need to turn continually to the subject of justification.

God's justifying work in Christ is the best and most effective remedy against the idolatry of relying on ourselves and falling into the trap of believing that it is what we *do* that identifies and establishes us before God. Justification rightly understood points us to the One through whom we are counted righteous by God, not on the basis of anything *we* do, whether past, present, or future, but on the basis of *his* perfect life, death, and resurrection for us.

Ultimately, justification is not about us but about Christ. It is about what he endured and accomplished on our behalf so that we might be made right with God. To be right with God, we must turn from ourselves and by faith lay hold of him who was raised for our justification.

The Aim of This Book

The goal throughout this book is to trace the basic contours of justification in the Bible from Adam to Abraham, through Israel, and into the New Testament. However, as a glance at the table of contents will show, this does not mean following justification in a straight line through the main eras of redemptive history. While the chapters do move forward from Adam, they do so, particularly in the first half of the book, in a cyclical way. So, for instance, the chapter on Adam is followed by a chapter on Christ as the second Adam. In this way, the events in the garden, particularly Adam's disobedience, are followed directly by a study of Christ, with particular focus on his obedience. So the two primary covenantal heads, one the head of the human race and the other the head of the new covenant, are considered side by side without recounting the entire Old Testament history that lies between them. Similarly, the chapter on Abraham in the Old Testament is followed by a chapter on Abraham and justification in the New Testament. The chapter on the righteousness required but not provided in the Mosaic law is followed by a chapter that explores some of the central New Testament texts that speak to how God's gift of righteousness in Christ becomes ours by faith.

The benefit of such an approach is that we may study how particular concepts flow together from both the Old Testament and the New Testament without leaving large gaps in the basic narrative of the book. The idea for such an approach is not particularly novel, but over the course of a few years of teaching justification in seminary classes, in Sunday school, and overseas with pastors and students, following this outline has proved helpful for tying together the various biblical strands related to justification.

The Motivations behind This Book

Besides my students, nothing has influenced the writing of this book more than my experience of teaching the Bible to pastors and students living in South and East Asia and engaging people in those regions, and here at home, who represent other major world religions. I spend time every year on short-term mission trips and have found that justification is not just a Western concern. Emphases may differ, cultural and historical factors may to a degree shape the way that justification is cast, and the doctrine may need contextualizing apart from the various figures associated with the justification debates swirling within the Western church since Luther, but the core issues remain front and center. This includes, by the way, the issues that lie perpetually at the heart of justification debates. For instance, I have found that questions about the grounds upon which God accepts people, whether the work of Christ is all-sufficient for our justification, what role our works play in our standing before God, and how justification fits into a larger understanding of salvation are not particularly Western or Eastern questions. I am more than aware of and sensitive to the differences that exist between Christians north and south of the equator, or between Christians east and west, but the basic question of how sinful human beings can stand before God without fear of judgment is neither culturally nor historically bound. The question may be clothed in different terms and circumstances, and a whole host of various cultural, social, and religious factors may influence how the question is framed, but it is *the question* that needs to be answered in every corner of the world in every generation.

The question is universal and transcends culture and history because the basic human condition is universal and transcends culture and history. Whoever we are, wherever we come from, whoever our ancestors may have been, we are by nature (fallen human nature) apt to rely on our works and accomplishments for our ultimate, even eschatological, well-being. That is who we are; we all inherited that from our common father, Adam. Whether people are rich or poor, democratic or theocratic, religious or secular, pleasant neighbors or suicide bombers only changes the ways and means by which ultimate ends are pursued. Similarly, whether from Muslim, Hindu, or Buddhist backgrounds, all share the same mortal illness found among Protestants, Catholics, Eastern Orthodox, and, for that matter, atheists and secular humanists: a universal love of idolatry in some form or another. Ultimately all idolatry is a matter of works and self-reliance, and everyone without exception is an idolater. You do not need a statue or a talisman to be an idolater; all you need is to be a child of Adam, and it will come naturally. That realization shaped and motivated the writing of this book.

Second, I have heard numerous pastors and students express a desire for a book that can help serve as an entryway into the larger discussion of justification in the Bible. In seminary classes and in churches, I am often asked to recommend books that present basic, biblical teaching on justification. There are several such works that are excellent, but it seemed to me that a book that takes a biblical-theological approach to justification and that takes little for granted in terms of background study, theological tradition, or knowledge of controversies would make a contribution to the larger discussion.[3]

This book, like the Explorations in Biblical Theology series in general, is written with an eye fixed on where the topic is most vital: in pulpits and churches. I sincerely hope that pastors preaching through biblical books and texts associated with justification, preaching justification topically, or preaching their way through the big picture of the Bible will find the material in these pages helpful for their own study, reflection, and preparation. I also hope that Bible students interested in studying justification—whether they are in formal classroom settings or not—will find that this book helps them get their foot in the door of studying the doctrine upon which the church, it is often said, stands or falls. This is a broad and potentially presumptuous goal, but it is what I set out to accomplish. It remains up to the reader to judge to what degree the goal is met.

Writing in a Climate of Debate

Controversy is nothing new to the doctrine of justification. Although Paul's doctrine of justification is certainly not limited to letters written in the midst of controversy, it is in those early controversies that he goes into the most detail. In Paul's letter to the churches in Galatia, beset by Judaizers seeking to add aspects of the law to requirements for salvation in Christ, justification is central. Likewise, writing to the Romans in a context in which there was some confusion or tension over the relationship between Jews and Gentiles, Paul again emphasizes justification. We should also note that Romans is not just a letter about Jew and Gentile relations; it also introduces Paul and much of his core theology to people who had not yet met him. It should get our attention that in such a letter Paul has much to say about what it means to be righteous before God.

3. See the Select Resources at the back of the book for examples of helpful works on justification.

Justification has remained a hot-button topic for much of church history, including today. Whether engaging the New Perspective on Paul in general, or focusing on individual writers who deny the traditional view of the imputation of Christ's righteousness and/or present a formidable recasting of the biblical story of justification, much of the literature published in the last several years by writers from a Reformational background aims to defend traditional views of justification. Just as important, several works have been published that carefully distinguish the differences between views associated broadly with traditional Reformed and Lutheran traditions and views that are either modified forms of those traditions or, in a few cases, stand outside Protestantism altogether (from people loosely in the "Protestant" tradition).

When I began writing this book some years ago, I also set out to write primarily in response to others with whom I disagree. Ironically, I never had a strong desire to write another response book and was not personally very interested in doing so, but I felt as if that approach was required if I were going to write a book on justification. Finally, my lack of desire to write such a book was met with encouragement from various people who expressed a wish for a book on justification that was not primarily polemical (i.e., against contrary views). As a result, I do not devote either chapters or major sections to direct engagement in the contemporary debates.

Just to be clear: I am not saying that this book is written in a vacuum, outside time and space and apart from the debates— it is just not primarily *in* the debates. To be sure, many of the emphases found here are clearly influenced from the context and climate in which they are written, and the debates are undoubtedly beneath the surface of this book in several places, but that is not the focus. Readers familiar with the controversies will hear their echoing, at times loudly, in various places. For instance, when I assert that it is impossible to deny the concept of works righteousness in Paul's description of himself as a zealous persecutor of the church and as one who had his own "righteousness" apart from Christ in Philippians 3, I do so in part as a response to contemporary claims to the contrary. There are also, of course, times when I address specific issues and individuals, but for the most part the driving idea behind this book is to set forth the foundational truths of justification from an unapologetically traditional Reformational perspective as they arise from Scripture. It is my prayer that I have accomplished something of what I set out to do between the covers of this book.[4]

4. There is some material here that overlaps with my book *Jesus' Blood and Righteousness* (Wheaton, IL: Crossway, 2006). That book deals specifically with the imputation of Christ's righteousness, and this book focuses more generally on justification, but it was inevitable that many of the biblical texts studied in that book (e.g., Rom. 4:1–8; 5:12–21; 2 Cor. 5:17–21; Phil. 3:8–10) would appear here too. When those texts come up in the course of this book, I often refer readers to specific sections in *Jesus' Blood*. I realize that doing so runs the risk of giving the impression that it is necessary to read that book first, but that is certainly not the case. I tried to keep such references to a minimum, and they are meant only to point readers to the more detailed and technical exegesis that lies behind many of the conclusions and assertions found here.

The Legacy of Adam

THIS CHAPTER CONSIDERS the biblical-theological themes in the story of Adam that directly impact the larger study of justification. The beginning, however, is read from the standpoint of the end. So while this chapter focuses on Adam, what follows is based on the whole scope of the Bible. We could wall off later revelation found in the Bible, but that is not, in my opinion, the typical way that Christians should read the Old Testament. We should read the Old Testament as those who are members of the new covenant established by the second Adam. We are bound to read the entire Bible in its specific canonical, historical, and redemptive contexts, including our own new covenant context.

Here are the focal points.

- Creator and Creature
- God and Man
- The End and the Beginning

Creator and Creature

Genesis 1:26–28 answers many of life's ultimate questions. How did I get here? Who am I? What am I? What am I supposed to do? There may be more to the answers than what is in these verses, but not less. Most importantly, this text tells us what we need to know fundamentally about ourselves and our relationship with God. It can be narrowed down to one word found in verse 27: "created." That may not seem like a groundbreaking observation, but we have a long track record of forgetting, denying, and militating against this most basic thing about our being. Consider this: our collective habit of forgetting or ignoring this basic truth lies at the root of every problem from Adam on down. It is no exaggeration to say that *every* sin begins with a refusal to accept this truth about ourselves. Whether we acknowledge it or not, we are *creatures* and not the Creator. Contrary to what we so often seem to want to believe, we are not independent, autonomous beings. We are creatures, created in the image of God. In other words, our life is, from the beginning, not strictly our own.

Dependence and Purpose

Beginning with a solid grasp of the fact that we are creatures, not the Creator, brings our lives into focus. We are created beings made to be absolutely dependent on God. This is how we were designed. Our dependence on God is further evidenced when we consider that God also designed our purpose in life. All human creativity, gifts, and abilities were given to us to fulfill our appointed task. In other words, we received the gift of life *and* the gift of work (cf. Gen. 2:15). Typically, discussion of the commands in the garden is limited to the negative command ("you will not") concerning the Tree of Knowledge of Good and Evil (2:17), but this misses an important part of the picture. The responsibilities that God gives Adam in 1:28 are commands. In his created innocence, Adam has positive commands to fulfill, and even though the entire creation was "good," it is not static. There is movement and purpose built into it. The creation, with humanity at the center, is going somewhere. God says to his creatures, "Have children, tame the earth, and rule over it." There is work to be done in this good creation. It appears from the outset that there is a goal to reach. Presumably the earth could reach a state of being filled, tamed, and ruled. A divinely appointed goal is woven into creation.

12

A Goal from the Beginning. We tend to think of eschatology as only the "end times" that wind up when Christ returns, but that is not all there is to it. Geerhardus Vos was right to refer to "pre-redemptive Eschatology."[1] Before the fall of Adam and the subsequent unfolding of redemption, there was an end for which God created the world. We need to be crystal clear on this—it is not the case that God had one plan before the fall and then a backup plan afterward. "God forbid," as Paul would say. There is, and I am not the first person to say it, no "plan B" in the Bible. There was and continues to be one end goal woven into the fabric of creation. Of course, at this precise point in the biblical narrative we do not yet see that the planned end point of creation will be summed up in another Adam (see Eph. 1:10). The goal we see at this point in the narrative is life. This goal is symbolized in the Tree of Life (Gen. 2:9) and, together with the outward trajectory of subduing and reigning over the world, the narrative implies that life *eternal* is the ultimate goal. Later we will find that the goal and promise of life is attached to obedience in the Mosaic law, will be announced by the prophets, and will be attained finally in the second Adam.

God and Man

A special kind of history begins in Genesis 2. What I mean is that Genesis 2 refocuses the historical narrative on the creation of humanity, the particular place we have in the created order, and especially the special relationship that exists between us and God. Genesis 2:4 picks up and expands the story that began in 1:1 and then unfolds through the rest of Scripture and beyond. Unlike anything in the rest of creation, the text places special emphasis on God's creation of mankind: "Then the LORD God formed the man of dust from the ground and breathed into his

---

1. As Vos says, "It is not biblical to hold that eschatology is a sort of appendix to soteriology. . . . The universe, as created, was only a beginning, the meaning of which was not perpetuation, but attainment." Geerhardus Vos, *The Eschatology of the Old Testament*, ed. James T. Dennison Jr. (Phillipsburg, NJ: P&R Publishing, 2001), 73.

nostrils the breath of life, and the man became a living creature" (2:7). What jumps off the page of Scripture is the sovereignty of God the Creator and the dependence of man his creature upon him. The ways and means of the creation of man should get our attention. Adam is formed from the dirt and given life by God himself. God creates a special place for Adam to live, a garden from which he is to fulfill the creation mandate of 1:28 (2:8). This is also a place where Adam enjoys unique fellowship with God (see 3:8). Adam the creature dwells in the creation in fellowship with the Creator. This will not be the last time in Scripture when people, land, and God are linked together. God provides everything that Adam needs for life and happiness. Not only do the trees around him provide fruit, they are also "pleasant to the sight" (2:9). Then we are told of two special trees—the Tree of Life and the Tree of Knowledge of Good and Evil. So God sculpts Adam into form, breathes him into existence, and sets him to work (v. 15).

The Covenant God

In chapter 2, a change takes place that has repercussions for how we read this narrative. In chapter 1 the Hebrew word "God" (*Elohim*) is typically used, but after the initial account of God's creative work comes to an end in 2:3, his special covenant name "LORD" (*Yahweh*) is also used. Bearing in mind that the first hearers/readers of this text were Israelites under the Mosaic covenant, it is striking that when the text of Genesis turns to focus particularly on the creation of man and his relationship with God, the name of God is precisely that covenant name later revealed to Moses on Sinai (Ex. 34:6). Genesis 2 spells out God's care for Adam in more detail, including the planting of Eden where Adam would enjoy special communion with God and the provision of food to sustain Adam's life. All the good gifts come specifically from "the LORD God" (*Yahweh Elohim*). The God of creation, the God who created Adam, is the God with whom Israel has a covenantal relationship.

Setting the Boundaries

In the midst of paradise there is one thing forbidden, and it is mentioned along with a threat that seems out of place in the pastoral scene of Eden.[2] Adam may eat from any tree except one, and God warns Adam that if he eats of the Tree of Knowledge of Good and Evil, he will die (2:17). The story is about creation, life, and abundance, but a foreign and future enemy appears, and with it a challenge confronts Adam. In paradise, in his created innocence, Adam is given a command, and a curse is attached to it in the case of disobedience. Death is God's condemnation for disobedience. Adam must obey perfectly or he will die.

Adam's "Probation." Sometimes Adam's situation in Eden is referred to as *probation*. That is, Adam was put in Eden for a period during which he needed to prove himself through obedience and maintain his innocence until he reached or was granted a perfected, glorified state of being. For nearly everyone living in the twenty-first century, the word *probation* has negative associations. Probation is typically something one is put on after committing a crime. Someone charged with a crime may be given probation, or a prisoner may be granted probation to see if he can make it on the outside. Innocent citizens are not on probation. About the only time we speak of a probationary period apart from the idea of guilt or offense is when we are offered a trial period to sample a product, although we do not call that probation. Theologians of earlier generations could use *probation* and expect readers to understand their meaning, but English usage has changed, and with it the word *probation* has a more narrow use. Someone might object that technical language in any field, not least in theology, must always be explained. However, the word *probation* itself was the explanation used to describe Adam's situation in Eden. This is simply not true today. Modern people might hear the word *probation* and easily think that Adam was somehow created guilty, or at

2. James Montgomery Boice's description of chapter 2's casting "shadows over Eden" is fitting. He points out that in the midst of all the good things—relationship with God, a garden in which to live and work, and a wife—"there are forebodings." *Genesis, Volume 1: Creation and Fall* (Grand Rapids: Baker, 1998), 113.

least think him suspect. But Adam was innocent, and that is a vital part of the story. Is there a word that better captures Adam's situation in the garden? There is, but to prove it we have to expand our biblical vision past Genesis and note a particular pattern that arises and helps us to understand Adam's circumstances in the garden.

Testing—a Biblical Pattern. The better alternative to *probation* is *test*. Granted, the word does not appear in the text, but there is a pattern here that can be seen throughout Scripture. In the Bible, obedience to God is not taken for granted. God gives commands and then tests the obedience of those who receive the commands. At pinnacle points in Scripture, obedience is tested because obedience, which means submitting to God and acting on his command (including not eating fruit), displays one's trust in and loyalty to God. Testing may also reveal distrust and disloyalty. In three crucial eras in the biblical revelation of God's salvation, he tests his servants. God tests Abraham, Israel, and finally his own Son, Jesus. Although the tests have varying results, they are all tests for obedience.

"Now I Know You Fear God." Abraham is associated with many things, but in the discussion of justification, he is best known for his faith: "And he believed the LORD, and he counted it to him as righteousness" (Gen. 15:6). There is also a well-known time in Abraham's life when God tested him. In Genesis 22, God tells Abraham to take his only beloved son, the son of the promise, to Mount Moriah and to sacrifice him as a burnt offering (vv. 1–2). Far and away the emphasis in the text is on Abraham's obedience. We will return to this scene later, but for now it is enough to note that Abraham's inner struggle as he trudged up the mountain to sacrifice his son is not on display, but his obedience to God. We are told that Abraham woke up the next day, made preparations, and set out on his journey. Of course, his faith is on display too when he tells his servants that he and Isaac will return (v. 5) and when he tells Isaac that God will give them a lamb for the offering (v. 8). The interconnection of faith and obedience is clear. But again, it is obedience that is on display. As the knife is about to fall, Abraham hears the angel of the Lord telling him to stop: "Do not lay your

hand on the boy or do anything to him" (v. 12). Then we hear the reason for the intervention and, I believe, the reason for the entire episode: "for now I know that you fear God, seeing you have not withheld your son, your only son, from me." Abraham passed the test. Then the promises of chapters 12, 15, and 17 are repeated (vv. 16–18). The declaration of Abraham's righteousness by faith was no empty proclamation (15:6). Abraham's obedience on Moriah displays his faith and also proves that what God declared is true.

"That I May Test Them." The story of Israel is marked by testing. In the wilderness and in the land, God tests them to see what is in their hearts. He tests them with the manna: "Behold, I am about to rain bread from heaven for you, and the people shall go out and gather a day's portion every day, that I may test them, whether they will walk in my law or not" (Ex. 16:4 ESV). Of course, this is again a test of faith—the Israelites must believe that God will daily provide for them. If they gather more than a day's manna, they imply that God cannot be trusted. Disobedience flows from a lack of faith. However, the *explicit* emphasis in the text is on obedience, for it is by their actions that their hearts are revealed. Their whole experience in the wilderness is a test: "And you shall remember all the way which the LORD your God has led you in the wilderness these forty years, that He might humble you, *testing you*, to know what was in your heart, whether you would keep His commandments or not" (Deut. 8:2 NASB). Later, after entering the Promised Land and continuing in the disobedience that marked their forty years of wandering, God becomes angry with them and says, "Because this nation has transgressed My covenant which I commanded their fathers, and has not listened to My voice, I also will no longer drive out before them any of the nations which Joshua left when he died, *in order to test Israel* by them, whether they will keep the way of the LORD to walk in it as their fathers did, or not" (Judg. 2:20–22 NASB). This pattern of testing is well documented in Israel's history, as is the fact that they failed the majority of the time.[3]

3. Other texts with explicit references to testing are Ex. 20:20; Deut. 8:16; 13:3; 2 Chron. 32:31. There are also references to God's testing people in general: Ps. 11:4; Jer. 20:12.

"If You Are the Son of God." Outside paradise, in the wilderness, God tested the obedience of his Son, Jesus Christ. It is true that he was tempted by Satan, but Matthew and Luke make it clear that the Devil didn't prompt the testing: "Then Jesus was *led* up by the Spirit into the wilderness *to be* tempted by the devil" (Matt. 4:1; cf. Luke 4:1–2). Like Israel, Christ's test takes place in the wilderness. Unlike Adam and Israel, Christ is tested and passes.

The close connection of Jesus with the tests of Adam and Israel is evident in the New Testament. Luke draws the line from Christ back to Adam by ending his genealogy with "Adam, the son of God" (3:37). Then, immediately after the genealogy, with Adam fresh in the readers' minds, the temptation narrative begins. Matthew begins his gospel by tracing Jesus' lineage back to Abraham and spends three chapters showing that Jesus is the fulfillment of the promises to Israel. After establishing that Jesus is the Messiah, the one to whom the prophets pointed, the narrative of Jesus' adult life and ministry begins. He is baptized by John, affirmed by the Father ("this is my beloved Son, with whom I am well pleased"—3:17), and ushered out to be tested in the wilderness.[4]

Adam was put in the garden with a command placed upon him, and soon after the command was given, Adam's obedience to that command was tested. This sets a pattern that extends through Scripture: God tests his children to see whether they will obey him. There are tests connected to every major chapter of the history of redemption, culminating with the accepted and beloved Son of God (Matt. 3:17; Mark 1:11; Luke 3:22). So, the idea behind the concept of *probation* is affirmed, but better explained today with the simple word *test*, or if we want to be a little more exacting, *test period*.

There is a similar mention of testing obedience in the New Testament as well. Paul tells the Corinthians that he wrote to them so "that I might test you and know whether you are obedient in everything" (2 Cor. 2:9).

4. Luke bookends his genealogy with the affirmation from heaven (3:22) and the temptation narrative (4:1–13). In this way Jesus' role as an obedient, acceptable son is emphasized, 3:22 ending with "you are my beloved son" and 3:38 ending with "Adam, the son of God." As the new Adam, Jesus obeys when tested and thus affirms the acceptance proclaimed by the Father.

The Question of "What If?" Talk of a test period often raises a question about the length of time that Adam was to be tested before he officially passed. It is important to address this question before proceeding. The answer to the question "What if Adam had obeyed?" usually goes something like this: he would have been granted that state of perfection due his perfect performance of God's standard. The idea is that Adam and his descendants would have reached that place of glorification that now will come to those who have faith in Christ.

The "if Adam had obeyed" question is driven by the recognition that a goal is built into creation. It is also a hypothetical question meant to help us think through and understand the implications of the larger biblical teaching in regard to what Christ, the second Adam, accomplished. But however much the inference is a fair one, it is important that we remember that the *real goal* was never for the human race to be perfected in Adam (no plan B!). The question may have some theological benefit, but we have to be careful of the unbiblical implication that if Adam had obeyed, he and his children would have been perfected in and through him—apart from Christ. As far as Scripture goes, the theological hypothetical does not play much of a role in the unfolding of redemption in Christ—except that Adam's failure to obey sets the necessary scene for the obedience of the one for whom Adam serves as a type (Rom. 5:14). Perhaps the question of Adam's obedience can be addressed in this way: "He didn't obey, and that is precisely the point. God's goal was not in Adam but in another through whom the people of God would truly be perfected and reach their appointed goal."[5]

The Question of Covenant

There were two parties in the garden—God and man. Of course, the Serpent is there too, but he is not part of the particular relationship between God and Adam. It is not an equal partnership; God is superior and Adam is inferior. God is independent and

5. According to Paul, God's plan was always Christ (Eph. 1:10).

JUSTIFICATION BY GRACE THROUGH FAITH

Adam is dependent. God provides everything that Adam and Eve need for life and happiness, but this is not a relationship without specific stipulations. God, the Creator and provider, establishes rules for maintaining the relationship. Adam is ordered to carry out his work of subduing and ruling the creation over which God has placed him. There is, however, a condition—there is one tree, and one tree only, from which Adam may not eat. The Tree of Knowledge of Good and Evil is forbidden with a warning. God tells Adam that he can eat from all the other trees, but if he eats from the one forbidden tree, "in the day that you eat of it you shall surely die" (Gen. 2:17). Implicit in the warning (and symbolized in the Tree of Life) is the promise that if Adam does not eat from the one tree, he will live. God sets life and death before Adam, as he will later with the Israelites in their covenant context: "See, I have set before you today life and good, death and evil" (Deut. 30:15). If Adam wants to live in his relationship with God, he must keep God's command. These words apply to Adam: "Therefore choose life, that you and your offspring may live" (Deut. 30:19). Here in the garden, before the fall, yet another biblical pattern is established. Later on, this kind of relationship gets a specific name: covenant.

There is much debate over whether the relationship between God and Adam can properly be called a covenant; after all, the word *covenant* does not appear until Genesis 6. Given the number of times the word will appear later, what stopped Moses from using the word here? After all, God tells Noah that he is making a covenant (6:18) and likewise tells Abraham explicitly that he is establishing a covenant (17:7), so why not here? Although it is not much of a stretch to think that the first people to hear and read Genesis, themselves living in a covenant, would have recognized a covenant when they saw one, it is a fair question. Perhaps formal covenants, like the Noahic, Abrahamic, Mosaic, and new covenants, are fitted for a redemptive context. That is, they are specific relationships between God and people, at times established on the basis of or formalized in blood, that aim at reestablishing the relationship broken in Eden. Perhaps it is enough

20

to say that the relationship between God and Adam foreshadowed what would later be called a covenant. John Murray, for instance, opted for "Adamic Administration,"[6] which ties together the idea that there is indeed a special relationship between God and Adam with the fact that *covenant* does not explicitly appear. In spite of the difficulties, are there good reasons for thinking that God and Adam were in a covenantal relationship? There are at least four reasons that suggest a covenant in Eden.[7]

Covenants Are Not Just Redemptive. The absence of the word *covenant* is not necessarily as strong an argument as it appears. True, there is no sacrifice to establish or commemorate the relationship between God and Adam; on the other hand, nothing like that was needed. In the Mosaic and new covenants, blood was required to bring God and man together because humanity stood under God's wrath due to their sin. Only the blood of a sacrifice, and ultimately only one sacrifice, could fulfill God's justice. With Abraham, God establishes a covenant in which he makes an oath, symbolized in sacrifices (Gen. 15:9–18), to keep his promise to make Abraham a great nation. These covenants contain sacrifices because they are redemptive, but the fact that they are redemptive *is not what makes them covenants.* They are special types of covenantal relationships between God and man connected to the Bible's big picture of reestablishing a people set apart for God so that they will be his people and he will be their God.[8] They are, at heart, covenantal relationships because they contain agreements, promises, and warnings between the two

6. John Murray, *The Collected Writings of John Murray*, vol. 2 (Carlisle, UK: Banner of Truth, 1977), 47–59.

7. For an insightful and concise discussion of the question of a covenant in Eden, see J. V. Fesko, *Justification: Understanding the Classic Reformed Doctrine* (Phillipsburg, NJ: P&R Publishing, 2008), 112–22.

8. This refrain, or something similar to it, is found in every covenantal era. For instance, in Leviticus the phrase is used as a promise for what will be fulfilled if Israel obeys (26:12); in Jeremiah it is the reality promised in the new covenant (31:33)—and it is taken up as fulfilled by both Paul (2 Cor. 6:16) and the writer to the Hebrews (Heb. 8:10). The last time these words are heard in the Bible is when John sees a vision of the new heaven and new earth (Rev. 21:3). The idea in the refrain is implicit everywhere in the Abrahamic covenant, with God promising to be with Abraham and his children and make them into a great nation (Gen. 12:2; 18:18).

parties involved in each relationship. Although God has something greater than Eden in store for humanity, the relationship in Eden is the model for the goal of redemption and the restoration of the relationship between God and humanity.

Christ the Head of the New Covenant. Second, the relationship established by and on Christ the second Adam is a covenant. It is the "new covenant in my blood," as he told his disciples on the night that he was betrayed (Luke 22:20). The apostle Paul presents Christ as a second Adam who stands as the head of God's people (Rom. 5:12–19; 1 Cor. 15:21–22). As Adam represented humanity, and as the consequence of his actions flowed to his race, so Christ stands as representative for those who believe and are counted righteous as a consequence of his actions. The writer to the Hebrews speaks at length of the new covenant, promised by the prophets (e.g., Jer. 31:33) and mediated by Christ (Heb. 8:13; 9:15; 12:24).

Hosea 6:7. In the context of Hosea 6, the prophet is speaking against the sins of Judah and Ephraim. In the midst of it we read these words: "But like Adam they transgressed the covenant; there they dealt faithlessly with me" (Hos. 6:7). Readers of the ESV, NASB, and NIV might wonder why there is a question about this text since it says plainly, "like Adam" (*ke'adam*). The issue is how to translate the Hebrew behind "like Adam." The Septuagint translator of Hosea chose the Greek for "as man" (*'hws anthropos*), which is followed in English by the KJV and the NKJV.[9] There is also the possibility, which some Old Testament scholars prefer, that the word refers to the geographical location mentioned in Joshua 3:16. When the feet of the priests carrying the ark touched the Jordan River, its waters "stood and rose up in a heap very far away, at Adam, the city that is beside Zarethan."

Taking "Adam" to be the place mentioned in Joshua 3:16 is not impossible, although we then have to assume that there was a well-known, serious breach of the covenant there not recorded in the Old Testament. That fact in itself does not rule out this

9. The Septuagint, sometimes abbreviated LXX, is a Greek translation of the Hebrew Old Testament.

interpretation—it is not hard to imagine that there were significant acts of rebellion on Israel's part that are not mentioned in the Bible. It also fits with the inclusion of the word *sham* ("there") in the text. It is worth noting, however, that in the *one text* where this place is named (Josh. 3:16), the focus is all about God's faithfulness in bringing Israel to the Promised Land and his miraculous work of dividing the Jordan, not about Israel's covenant breaking.[10]

Reading it as "like man" or "mankind" is also possible.[11] The problem with this interpretation, however, is that it makes the word "there" difficult to understand. "Like man (or mankind) they transgressed the covenant; *there* they dealt faithlessly with me." The questions that remain unanswered in this interpretation are, Where is *there*? and How does *there* fit the context? The KJV and NKJV take it this way, but it is vague, to say the least.

Taking this verse to refer to Adam best fits the context of Hosea. True, this interpretation is not without problems, and it is certainly not accepted by everyone, but it does have the advantage of (1) referring to a known entity in the Bible, and (2) fitting the context of Hosea. There is still a problem with the word "there" referring back to a person, but it is not a great leap to infer that after mentioning the person Adam, Hosea refers to Eden. Second, the context of Hosea is all about Israel's unfaithfulness to the covenant in spite the "abundant generosity of God, who had loaded Israel down with all manner of good things."[12] Like Adam, God gave Israel everything they needed for life and well-being, including his own presence; yet, also like Adam, they chose their own way over God's good gifts and thereby transgressed the covenant.[13]

10. Another thing often brought up against the view that Hosea refers to the place mentioned in Joshua 3:16 is that the Hebrew preposition *ke* rarely means "at." This is not a very strong argument, however, because as long as it is possible for it to mean "at" (and it is possible), then the fact that it is rare is only suggestive and certainly not decisive.

11. Calvin, notably, read it this way. See, *Hosea*, Calvin Translation Society 13 (Grand Rapids: Baker, 1993), 235. Cited in Fesko, *Justification*, 117n21.

12. C. John Collins, "Adam and Eve in the Old Testament," *The Southern Baptist Journal of Theology* 15, 1 (Spring 2011): 16. Collins cites the following texts in Hosea as some examples of Israel's covenant breaking: 2:8–13; 7:15; 11:1–4; 13:4–6.

13. Choosing one's own way over against the way God provides and commands is also known as "works righteousness." More of that in later chapters, but like so many other biblical themes, works righteousness begins in Eden.

Covenantal Testing. The testing of Adam is the fourth thing that suggests a covenant in Eden. There is no need to repeat the discussion above, but like Abraham the covenant man, Israel the covenant nation, and Christ the covenant head, Adam's loyalty to God and his willingness to honor the relationship God established with him were tested.

The relationship established in Eden was covenantal. The evidence for it spans the Bible. At the very least the relationship between God and Adam in Eden suggests a covenant. In my view there is more than a suggestion—there is a sound biblical-theological conclusion. No doubt some people will remain unconvinced that an actual covenant is found here in Genesis because the word does not appear. Some Bible readers will continue to think that the idea of a covenant with Adam is a result of dedication to a larger theological system. And others will insist that covenants do not appear until after the fall when the biblical pattern of redemption unfolds—but I hope most will agree that the relationship between God and Adam in Eden sets the pattern for the relationships that will soon be called covenants in the Bible.

"You Can Be Like God": The First and Greatest Temptation

There is a classic rock song by Fleetwood Mac called "Go Your Own Way." That could have been the theme song of the first temptation in Eden.[14] God held nothing back from Adam and Eve. Everything, including one another, was theirs to enjoy. There was one thing, however, that they could never have nor could ever be, and that is exactly what Satan dangled in front of them. The Serpent is introduced as "more crafty than any other beast of the field that the LORD God had made" (Gen. 3:1), and he knew exactly how to tempt the first couple in ways they could not resist.

God's role as Creator, and the Serpent as both evil and a part of creation (a creation Adam was meant to rule over, not submit to), is emphasized as the temptation narrative begins.

---

14. For some, "My Way," made famous by Frank Sinatra, might be a better analogy.

The rebellion against God originates with a created being before Adam and Eve ate the fruit. What follows is a thinly veiled attack on God as the Serpent implicitly calls God a liar, "you will not surely die" (3:4); a deceiver, "God knows that when you eat of it your eyes will be opened" (v. 5); and an equal rather than their Creator, "you will be like God" (v. 5). The created Serpent tells the created woman that she and her created husband can be just like God. The tempter succeeds. Addled by the temptation, Eve skews God's revealed word and extends the prohibition against eating to include touching. The pace of the narrative hurtles toward the climactic moment that sets the future of the human race in motion: "When the woman saw that the tree was good for food, and that it was a delight to the eyes, and that the tree was to be desired to make one wise, she took of its fruit and ate, and she also gave some to her husband who was with her, and he ate" (v. 6). It takes only six verses to tell the story of the fall and just two verses to interpret what took place.

First, their eyes are opened, but not in the way that the Serpent had promised: "Then the eyes of both of them were opened, and they realized they were naked; so they sewed fig leaves together and made coverings for themselves" (v. 7, NIV). Then they find that rather than being God's equal, they are not even in the position granted to them in the original creation. Rather than enjoying the presence of their Creator, they hide from him when they hear him coming. Everything changes in the biblical narrative from this point.

Questions and Incriminations

"Where are you?" God calls to Adam. This is one of the most tragic lines in the biblical narrative. It is not tragic because God somehow cannot find them or does not know where they are; it is tragic because they must hide in guilt and shame. Well before the dialogue begins, Adam and Eve's position before God is evident. God knows what they have done, and when confronted with it (v. 11), the first blame game begins. The last time we heard from

Adam about Eve, he was singing her praises and declaring her as his one and only (2:23), but now he turns on her: "She gave it to me." Even worse, Adam not only blames Eve, he first implicates God and by doing so reveals the true depths of his newfound rebellion. He points his finger at God to try to shift blame to the one who is eternally blameless: "The woman whom you gave to be with me, she gave me fruit of the tree, and I ate" (3:12). Of course, Eve too shifts the blame: "the serpent deceived me, and I ate" (v. 13). No one takes responsibility; no one is righteous. Hatred of God and neighbor begins.

Evil has a foothold in the world, man is in rebellion against God, and by rights the story could end here. "In the day that you eat of it you shall surely die" was the word from God about the punishment for eating the forbidden fruit. Adam and Eve, how-ever, do not die, not immediately at least. God has a plan to make them and their children right again.

The End and the Beginning

The pastoral scene in Eden is destroyed by disobedience. Because of Adam's failure, he and his descendants will bear the curse of 2:17. God first curses the Serpent, and the curse includes an enigmatic promise to both the Serpent and to Eve's children. The defeat of the Serpent will come through the line of Eve (3:15). From this point on, curse and promise will flow together until, through a curse, the promise of God is fulfilled (Gal. 3:13–14).

Grace in the Curse

Genesis 3 introduces a central biblical theme that, like the word "covenant," is not stated explicitly. That theme is grace. Many have argued that the grace of God is implicit from Genesis 1:1. After all, God did not *have* to create the world; he did not *have* to create humanity and provide for them—it was all done by his grace. There is a general way that we can speak of creation as an act of grace. This is especially so if we view creation as ultimately inseparable from salvation, although typically when people refer to creation as an act of grace, I doubt that they have the whole complex of creation-fall-redemption-consummation in mind. We often use the word *grace* to signify what is sometimes called "common grace," that is, the general grace of God that sustains the human race apart from their belief in him and in spite of their ongoing rebellion against him. But not even the idea of "common grace"—connected as it typically is to God's general grace to humanity *after the fall*—really fits when applied to Genesis 1 and 2. "Grace" in the Bible, when applied particularly in the context of God's acts of salvation, is more than God's gift to neutral humanity. Christians often speak of "unmerited" or "unearned" favor to describe God's grace, and put that way it can be applied to God's act of creation. In the Bible, however, grace as it connects to salvation is not just *unmerited* but *de-merited* favor.

When the apostle Paul says we are "justified by his grace as a gift" (Rom. 3:24), he is not talking about the justification of the morally neutral who simply had done nothing to deserve God's favor. To the contrary, "all have sinned and fall short of the glory of God" (v. 23). In Romans 6:14, "grace" is contrasted with "sin." In Ephesians 2:5, it is those who were "dead in our trespasses" who were made "alive together with Christ." In Titus 3, those who "were foolish, disobedient, led astray, slaves to various passions and pleasures" are the ones "justified by his grace" (vv. 3, 7). There are plenty of times in the Bible, particularly in the New Testament, when the word "grace" is used in general ways, but in the context of God's saving acts it is applied to those who are morally broken, undeserving to receive God's favor because of their rebellion against him. Paul sums it up best when he says "while we were still sinners, Christ died for us" (Rom. 5:8), and goes on to describe us as at one time the enemies of God (v. 10). The backdrop for this is the "grace" in which those justified by grace stand (v. 2).

Grace as God's gift to morally corrupt humanity fits the context of Genesis 3. The seed of the woman will continue on and ultimately be the cause of the Serpent's destruction. Although it is only through the woman's pain, the human race will still multiply. Although imbalanced and at odds, man and woman will stay together. Although only by sweating in thorn-laden fields, the human race will still be sustained (3:17–19). Life goes on, although enveloped by a shadow, "till you return to the ground, for out of it you were taken; for you are dust, and to dust you shall return" (v. 19). Even their banishment from the garden is for their ultimate benefit. God sends Adam and Eve out of the garden to prevent their eating of the Tree of Life, presumably to keep them from living forever in a fallen state (v. 22). God has a plan for providing eternal life. Through disobedience the last enemy, death, enters the world. As the story unfolds, it becomes gradually clearer that only through obedience and death will death itself be destroyed and life restored.

Out of Eden: The Setting for the Rest of the Story

The opening chapters of Genesis set the scene for the rest of Scripture. Salvation, and consequently justification, cannot fully be understood apart from this. In three short chapters the story of the human race unfolds from bliss to destruction. In an act that may foreshadow sacrifice for covering man's sin, God clothes Adam and Eve. The curse is complete as God throws them out of Eden. The presence of God is now hidden from man, guarded, not for the last time, by angelic figures.[15] The first man and woman become the first exiles wandering the wilderness without God and without hope in the world.

Bridge to the Bible. There are two central figures in the Bible. Adam is one of them. Although other men receive far more attention (Abraham, Moses, and David, for example), none of them plays a role near that of Adam's. The figure of Adam stands over all of them; he is, one might say, the problem that will not go away. He explains why the human race plummets downward after him. He is the explanation for why people do not obey God when they are told explicitly what he wants them to do—after all, if Adam did

---

15. Think of the carved seraphim overshadowing the ark of the covenant.

not obey in his innocence, what is going to happen to people living under his curse when they are given commands from God? Adam explains sin and death—through his disobedience both come to the human race (Rom. 5:12; 1 Cor. 15:21–22). His act of disobedience determines the relationship of his children before God. We are, all of us, born outside Eden. There is, however, another figure, larger than Adam and yet also Adam. A second and last Adam. Adam is called "the son of God" (Luke 3:38), and this one is also called God's Son. But this one is a "beloved" Son who pleases his Father in every way and is accepted by him. As Adam's disobedience alienated his children from God, so will the second Adam's obedience be the way that will right that relationship. Through the first Adam we were made sinners; through the second we are made righteous. The next chapter follows that trajectory.

The Obedient Second
and Last Adam

THE FOCUS OF THIS CHAPTER is on the true Adam in whom we are made righteous before God. That is, we are deemed by God to be those who have done what is right in his eyes according to his divine standards. To be righteous before God means that God judges us to be without guilt and as those who have obeyed him in every way. The disobedience of the first Adam brought death and sin, but the obedience of the second Adam brings life and a righteous standing before God. Here are the central topics.

- Disobedience unto Death and Obedience unto Life
- From Sinners to Righteous
- Conclusion: Christ-Centered Justification

There are only two kinds of people in the world, those in Adam and those in Christ. Regardless of the vast differences in culture and ethnicity, philosophy and ethics, religion and morals, and however else humanity can be divided, everyone is either under the curse that fell on Adam or forgiven and accepted by God through Christ. It comes down to two men and how the disobedience of the one makes many "sinners" and the obedience of the other makes many "righteous" (Rom. 5:19). This is how the Bible, and Paul in particular, describes "all" humanity (Rom. 5:12, 18–19; 1 Cor. 15:21–22). Edward Fisher, speaking through the voice of

31

"Evangelista," rightly said that the apostle Paul in 1 Corinthians 15:47 speaks of Adam and Christ "as if there never had been any more men in the world besides these two; thereby making them head and root of all mankind, they having, as it were, the rest of the sons of men included in them."[1]

The story of the two Adams is the very foundation upon which the story of redemption unfolds. Everyone talks about stories these days, but this is truly *the* "big story" in the "big picture" of the Bible, and it can be followed forward and backward across Scripture. The aftermath of the first Adam flows beneath the accounts of Noah, Abraham, Jacob, David, and the life and experience of Israel. It is what leaves each of those stories incomplete; it is why there is no resolution in the Old Testament narrative. At the same time, the promise of the second Adam reverberates through the Old Testament, though often in no more than a whisper, and propels the grand narrative onward by holding out ultimate hope in the face of cyclical sin, failure, and deferred fulfillment.

Disobedience unto Death and Obedience unto Life (Rom. 5:12–21)

Context of Romans

Romans 5:12–21 is like a hub of a wheel—it is the center around which everything turns. At this point in Romans Paul has brought everything back to the beginning. From the famous words in 1:16–17, "I am not ashamed of the gospel . . . . For in the gospel the righteousness of God is revealed—a righteousness that is by faith from first to last, just as it is written: 'The righteous will live by faith.'" (NIV), Paul goes on to fill in the content of the gospel. The first section concludes with a string of Old Testament quotes that sums up the state of humanity. The quotes are book-

---

1. *The Marrow of Modern Divinity* (Ross-shire, UK: Christian Focus, 2009), 65.

ended with "There is no one righteous, not even one" (3:10 NIV) and "There is no fear of God before their eyes" (v. 18).

Paul is not just talking about sinfulness in general, nor is he just making observations about the human condition; he establishes God's case against humanity. Before the holy judge, everyone is condemned. Paul is not content simply to show from experience and example alone that both Jews and Gentiles have failed to live up to God's righteousness. He calls the law as Exhibit A to prove beyond a shadow of doubt that God's contention against humanity is just. The condemning function of the law is clear in many parts of the Bible, but nowhere is it more so than in Romans 3:19–20.

Universal Guilt Proven through the Law

The law, through which no one can be justified and through which comes the knowledge of sin (3:20), serves to prove the guilt of all people before God. The accountability of all is seen through the Jews' experience with the law. When Paul says that "the law speaks to those under the law," he means the Jews who had the Mosaic law. The law that speaks to the Jews is the same law that shuts down any idea of Gentile innocence before God and that holds the entire world, both Jewish and Gentile, responsible. This text can be difficult to understand, and someone might say, "How can I, with no known Jewish blood or ancestry, be condemned by a law that I and my ancestors never had?" What Paul means is this: the law spelled out what is needed to be righteous before God, and the consequences of obedience and disobedience. No one in Israel had to wonder about God's desires or commands. But even with that clear expression of God's will for their lives, the nation did not obey. When the Jews who had the law did not keep it, their hearts were revealed. The Gentiles have this same heart. So, if those who live under the law show themselves unable and unwilling to keep the law, then what hope can there be for those outside the law? In this way, the law establishes the accountability of everyone to God. There is solidarity between Jews and Gentiles.

Then Paul gives God's solution to humanity's plight: a right relationship with God comes through faith in Christ, in whom is revealed God's judgment and salvation, his righteousness (3:21–31). The idea of justification by faith is not a new invention; it was revealed ages earlier in the story of Abraham, father of the Jews. Abraham was not justified by works but by faith *in* the God who promised to make him a great nation and to bless the world through him. By believing, Abraham was counted righteous before God. He stood in a right relationship with God, his sins forgiven as a gift from God apart from works (4:1–8).

The story line of the Bible, however, reaches back beyond Abraham to the source of universal condemnation. There is a problem that must be dealt with because everyone, whether Abraham, Israelite, or Gentile, is under condemnation. Humanity's problem has a name: Adam. Although Paul establishes the once-for-all sacrifice of Christ that turns away God's wrath, forgives sin, and justifies (3:24–25), there is an underlying foundation without which justification by faith would be impossible. If what Paul says in 3:21–4:25 is true, then God has met the problem of Adam head-on and solved it for good.[2] So Paul draws the story of the Bible back to the beginning to establish the foundation of righteousness—the obedience of Christ that overturns the disobedience of Adam, defeats death and sin, and brings the gift of life.

Death and Sin through Adam

Death is the common denominator for all people. Through Adam, sin found its way into the world, and it was his sin that brought death (5:12).[3] Death and sin make up the two-part condition in which everyone after Adam enters the world. In my view,

---

2. I'm not the first to note this point: "If God has now been true to the promises to Abraham, it must mean that the long entail of sin and death has been overcome." N. T. Wright, *Justification: God's Plan and Paul's Vision* (Downers Grove: IVP, 2009), 226.

3. The question here is how to translate the Greek phrase, *eph' hō*. It is often taken for granted that it means "because," but there are good reasons against taking it that way. I have shown all the exegetical steps that lead to my conclusions about this text as well as the various interpretations of it in detail in *Jesus' Blood and Righteousness* (Wheaton, IL: Crossway, 2006), 123–41.

the best way to read verse 12 is this: "Therefore, just as through one man sin came into the world, and death came through sin, so in this way death spread to all men, *on account of which* all sinned." Adam's sin resulted in death (just as God warned in Gen. 2:17), but before he sinned death was not in the world. That condition existed only for Adam. For his children, death stands as a precondition for life. Everyone after Adam is born over a grave.

Because death, speaking specifically here of death as the condemnation for Adam's sin, reigns in the world, everyone sins. This interpretation runs a little against the grain of common translations and the view of many interpreters, which use the word "because" to translate the last part of verse 12. The usual reading is, "and so death spread to all *because* all sinned." Most interpreters would agree that the essential meaning of the text does not hinge on this phrase; however, I believe that Paul is giving the condition and the reason why everyone sins rather than emphasizing *in this particular verse* that each person's sin results in death—a point he makes crystal clear in verses 13 and 14.

Paul's point in verse 12 is to establish that the original sin of Adam, committed in innocence in a world where death was a warning and not yet a reality, connects all people to him. Yes, we do follow him by sinning and dying—"for the wages of sin is death" (6:23)—but our dying is not just a result of our personal sin, it is a reality for each one of us before we leave the womb. Adam, our father according to the flesh, sets the world as we know and experience it in motion and we, his children, are bound to him and his punishment. Everyone shares in the condemnation of Adam's sin as though each one sinned in the garden of Eden. Many scholars and pastors from a Reformational background understand this to be so, and that is why the phrase "in Adam" appears so often in books and sermons on this text: "all sinned *in Adam*." Adding "in Adam" recognizes that Paul is emphasizing the solidarity of condemnation shared by Adam and his descendants. This does not diminish the personal guilt of each person or create a circumstance in which no one can fairly be held accountable for personal sin.[4] Furthermore, we tend to distinguish personal sin and Adam's sin in ways that do not seem to interest Paul, "for he never conceived of separating individual sin from Adam's."[5] If we grasp the depth of our connection to Adam, then we will understand that what is his, namely sin and death, is ours. Our personal sins bear witness to our connection with Adam's sin *and* to the punishment (death) that God brought on the world as a result. Paul's main focus in this text is not on us but on the two men whose actions affect everyone aligned with them.

No Exceptions

There are universal implications to what Paul says in these verses. He has already made it clear that the gospel is for both Jews and Gentiles (1:16–17), that both Jews and Gentiles stand under God's condemnation (3:19–20), and that God is equally the God of Jews and Gentiles and justifies both through faith (vv. 29–30). It is the disobedience of Adam that accounts for the status of all people before God, whether with or without the law. What was true of those living between Adam and Moses is true today for those living apart from God's revelation in Christ—there are no exceptions, whether or not you know Moses, or even if you are on a deserted island.

The Type of the One to Come. Yet Paul distinguishes between the first sin of Adam and the kind of sins committed before the law, and he does this for the sake of the parallel he is building between Adam and Christ. Those "who did not sin by breaking a command, as did Adam" (5:14, NIV), are the people who lived before the giving of the law. Their sin was not like Adam's in that they did not sin against specific known commands.[6] Although their sin was not "counted" as a transgression—that is, a direct violation of God's given commands—nevertheless

4. A quick glance back to 1:18–3:20 will confirm this.
5. Thomas R. Schreiner, *Romans*, Baker Exegetical Commentary on the New Testament (Grand Rapids: Baker, 1998), 290.
6. Craig S. Keener, *Romans*, New Covenant Commentary Series (Eugene, OR: Cascade, 2009), 75.

they suffered the penalty of God's condemnation that hangs over the world for Adam's sin. No one captures the point of this verse better than Adolph Schlatter: "Yet nothing that could be compared with Adam's fall happened among the early generations of humanity, for they were not given a divine commandment. Nevertheless they were not free from dying. Death was the absolute master against whom there is no resistance."[7] In other words, they paid the wages of sin. At first glance it may seem odd that Paul would add the comment about Adam's being "a type of the one who was to come" (v. 14), but the point is to bring the parallel and *contrast* between Adam and Christ into clearer focus.[8]

A minimal definition of a type is a person, event, or institution in Scripture that points to a future person, event, or institution that fulfills it. A type and what fulfills it (sometimes referred to as an antitype) do not have to match exactly at every level, but they do follow similar patterns at particular points. There is some textual relationship between a type and what fulfills it, as well as an elevation in the activity, significance, or purpose. Some people think that Scripture must identify something specifically as a type for it to be such (as is the case in v. 14), but an explicit identification of a type is not necessary. Broadly speaking, we can identify the exodus (event) as a type of the salvation we have in Christ that frees us from slavery to sin, and the temple (institution) and everything that went with it as a type(s) of both Christ's priestly office and his sacrificial death for sin. In both cases there are historical connections, similar patterns, and definitely an increase or elevation in the significance and purpose when fulfilled in Christ.

7. Adolph Schlatter, *Romans: The Righteousness of God*, trans. Siegfried S. Schatzmann (Peabody, MA: Hendrickson, 1995), 128–29.
8. It is vital to stress that this text is a parallel *and* contrast. Witherington's comments are on the mark: "Paul is not suggesting that Adam and Christ are alike in all respects, not even in the way they affect the race that flows forth from them. The point of comparison is simply that in both cases the act of one man had far-reaching consequences for all those who came after him. . . . In all other respects, and at some length in vv. 13–17, Paul wishes to distinguish Adam and Christ." Ben Witherington III, *Paul's Letter to the Romans: A Socio-Rhetorical Commentary* (Grand Rapids: Eerdmans, 2004), 146–47.

As the covenant head of the human race, Adam had commands to obey, but he violated God's command not to eat from one tree, and that brought sin and death into the world (v. 12). Paul's use of the word *type* here links Adam and Christ together at this exact point: a relationship similar to that between God and Adam in the garden exists between God the Father and Christ. Paul is not commenting on Adam as a type of Christ generally but in regard to his role as covenant head over his people. The implication is that in fulfillment of his role as the second Adam, Christ is to obey God's commands just as the "type" was meant to obey God's commands.

From the One to the Many

Paul develops the connection between Adam and Christ in the following verses by showing that through Christ, Adam's condemned children will reach God's intended fulfillment—they will "reign in life through the one man Jesus Christ" (v. 17). The goal of creation, unreached because of disobedience, is attained through the grace and gift that come from God through Christ. Recall that Adam's life in Eden was not static but moving toward a goal of life. That life, the promise of which was implied in the garden and symbolized in the Tree of Life, is made available through Christ's obedience (v. 19). It is through his life—his resurrected life—that we have life. The judgment of Adam's sin that brought condemnation is countered with the free gift that brings justification (v. 16) and eternal life (v. 21). Yet this is not a simple parallel. Christ's life and obedience is not some sort of salvific do-over. He obeyed in the wake of all the sin that followed on the heels of Adam. Death came through the disobedience of one man who lived in a state of created innocence. Life comes by way of a gift through God's grace that flows from Christ into a condemned and fallen world.

The Obedience of the Second Adam. Over against the "one trespass" that condemns all people (v. 18) and the "one man's disobedience" (v. 19) stands the "one act of righteousness" (v. 18) and "the one man's obedience" (v. 19). While it is not difficult to identify Adam's sin, there is debate about Christ's "one act of righteousness." While some assert that Paul has Christ's whole life in mind, others believe that the obedience is specifically his death on the cross. Given that Paul does call it "one act," it is most natural to take it as Christ's obedience to death on the cross. This does not, however, mean that the obedience that Christ performed in life can be separated from his obedience in death but that the cross stands as his decisive and supreme obedient act (cf. Phil. 2:8).[9] The vital aspect of these verses is that Christ's "righteous act" serves to "make many righteous." As the willful—one might say "active" —disobedience of Adam brought condemnation, so the obedience of Christ provides the foundation for the justification of Adam's children.

Obedience Is Active and Passive. The nature of Christ's obedience is at the center of what it means to be justified. Christ's obedience is sometimes divided between "active" and "passive" obedience. The idea is that Christ, as the second Adam and in contrast with the first Adam, obeyed the Father in life, and that *active* obedience is imputed to us. The cross, on the other hand, displays his *passive* obedience to the Father when he dies for the forgiveness of his people.[10] In churches that follow a general Reformational understanding of justification, it is common to hear something like, "We are justified by Christ's *active* obedience in life and his *passive* obedience in death," but that is not the way obedience pans out in the Bible. While the idea of the necessity for active and passive obedience is right, and sometimes convenient for theological discussion, it is practically impossible to separate obedience neatly into two parts.[11]

9. Douglas J. Moo, *Romans*, New International Commentary on the New Testament (Grand Rapids: Eerdmans, 1996), 344.

10. *Passive* does not mean *passivity*. Rather, it has to do with Christ's passion—his suffering on the cross.

11. As R. Scott Clark points out, the distinction is neither chronological nor between what Christ did and what was done to him, but rather: "Both adjectives are meant to describe, from different aspects, the entirety of Christ's work from the moment of his conception until the moment of his resurrection." "Do This and Live: Christ's Active Obedience as the Ground of Justification," in *Covenant, Justification, and Pastoral Ministry: Essays by the Faculty of Westminster Seminary California*, ed. R. Scott Clark (Phillipsburg, NJ: P&R Publishing, 2007), 230.

Since the Reformation, objections have been raised to the active obedience of Christ. Whatever the theological convictions of the various objectors, the concept of active obedience is often viewed as an intrusion to the Bible.[12] Most of those who reject active obedience view the forgiveness of sins as synonymous with justification. However, whether we unnaturally divide obedience into two distinct kinds (active=life; passive=death) or make the error of denying active obedience altogether, a similar problem exists: obedience, by its very nature, is simultaneously active and passive and cannot be separated; much less can one part be set aside. To obey means to submit to the will of the one who commands, but it also means that one must either *do* what is positively commanded or *not do* what is prohibited.

The nature of obedience is illustrated every day in parent-child relationships. For instance, when a father tells his son that he must mow the lawn before he can go to the swimming pool, the son, if he obeys, must submit to his father's will and put off going swimming until the grass is cut—but it *must* be cut, and sometimes twice depending on the effort put into the job. It is impossible to obey the command "passively" by submitting to the father's authority and will without also "actively" cutting the grass. Someone could reply that such an illustration oversimplifies the discussion, but the problem is not the simplicity of the illustration but the fact that a concept so easy to comprehend has been made overly complex by efforts to deny active obedience. Granted, it does not help matters when we provide fuel for its denial by making too much of a distinction between active and passive obedience, but if some people go a bit overboard at that point, this is not a reason for rejecting the idea. Arguing for active obedience is not a result of blindly following a particular confessional tradition or theological system; it is a biblical-theological and commonsense observation about the

---

12. I have traced various theological trajectories historically, taking special note of the type of emphasis or the denial of Christ's active obedience or "positive righteousness" in justification, in *Jesus' Blood and Righteousness*. See particularly 44–62. See also R. Scott Clark's historical overview of the active obedience of Christ in "Do This and Live," 230–41.

nature of obedience. Every act of obedience is, by necessity, both active and passive. The same is true of Christ's obedience—in life and in death. Christ's obedience *must* be understood as simultaneously active and passive. This becomes even clearer when Christ's obedience, as the second Adam, is considered in a covenantal context.

Covenantal Obedience of the Son

As Adam lived in a covenantal relationship with God, so too Jesus, in his role as second Adam and Son of God, relates to God his Father in what resembles a covenantal relationship.[13] True, with Christ no prohibition is given, nor is there a warning about the consequences of disobedience, but nonetheless a basic covenantal structure can be detected. Jesus speaks of himself in subordination to the Father, as acting in obedience to the commands of the Father, and as receiving eternal glory and inheriting eternal life for God's people through his obedience. In Eden, Adam is subordinate to God, has commands to carry out, and is promised life as an implied reward for his obedience. When Adam does not fulfill his obligations, a promise of another from the seed of Eve comes in the midst of the curse for disobedience (Gen. 3:15). As Bavinck puts it, "The Son appeared immediately after the fall, as Mediator, as the second and final Adam who occupies the place of the first, restores what the latter corrupted, and accomplishes what he failed to do."[14] The purposes of God unfold in Scripture through a series of covenants (with Adam, Noah, Abraham, Moses, David, and the new covenant), but the redemptive relationship between the Father and the Son is not merely a linear step in the series but the basis for the covenantally enacted plan of salvation.[15]

13. As Clark points out, "the biblical analogy between the First and Second Adams" is central to understanding a covenantal concept of redemption existing between the Father and the Son. R. Scott Clark, "The Covenant before the Covenants," in *Covenant, Justification, and Pastoral Ministry*, 189.

14. Herman Bavinck, *Reformed Dogmatics*, vol. 3, *Sin and Salvation in Christ*, ed. John Bolt, trans. John Vriend (Grand Rapids: Baker, 2009), 215.

15. Ibid.

A Covenant of Redemption(?). This conception of biblical redemption has given rise to identifying the relationship between the Father and the Son in redemption as a pact or agreement, i.e., a covenant made before creation. While many will balk at using the word "covenant" to describe an inter-Trinitarian relationship, when it comes to redemption Scripture does portray that relationship in terms of the Son's acting willingly in subordination to the Father to carry out his plan of salvation. This relationship is often called a "covenant of redemption." The very idea of a covenant of redemption or salvation, an eternal inter-Trinitarian pact for the salvation of God's people, will for some seem presumptuous, if not dangerous. Does not such a discussion lead us into places where angels, or human beings with even a hint of humility, should fear to tread? Yes, it can. But it need not do so. A biblical sense of fear ought to accompany discussion of *any* aspect of the person and/or works of God, but that fear should be applied more to answers than to questions. Although historically a kind of *covenant-a-mania* does exist, it is nevertheless worth asking whether theologians in the Reformed tradition were onto something biblical when speaking of a "covenant of redemption."[16] At the very least the concept is an acknowledgment that there was *some kind* of prior plan carried out by the Son in obedience to the Father. Most should be able to agree on that score, call it what we may. A brief consideration of a few related texts along with Romans 5 will help make the point.

The Witness of John. First, texts that speak more directly to Jesus' obedience imply a fulfillment of a prearranged plan, and also to the issue of "active" obedience. Several verses in John's Gospel highlight Jesus' intention to obey his Father's will, such as 4:34: "My food is to do the will of him who sent me and to accom-

16. As Vos, a supporter of the idea, points out, the covenant of redemption "has not always been defended too happily exegetically." Geerhardus Vos, "Doctrine of the Covenant in Reformed Theology," in *Redemptive History and Biblical Interpretation: The Shorter Writings of Geerhardus Vos* (Phillipsburg, NJ: Presbyterian and Reformed, 1980), 252. The discussion in Bavinck is concise yet well supported with Scripture. Writing from within the Reformed tradition, he is critical of the ways the idea has often been formulated but concludes that the *pactum salutis*, "despite its defective form, is rooted in a scriptural idea." *Reformed Dogmatics*, 3:214.

plish his work." Similarly, "For I have come down from heaven, not to do my own will but the will of him who sent me" (6:38).[17] While the emphasis in John 6 is ultimately on Jesus' death, it is unwarranted to limit Jesus' concern for doing his Father's will to the cross. In the same way, in 8:29, even though there is an emphasis on forgiveness (vv. 21, 24) and his impending crucifixion (v. 28), Jesus tells the Pharisees that the Father "has not left me alone, for I always do the things that are pleasing to him" (v. 29).

No text in John witnesses to the active and passive nature of obedience more than 10:18: "No one takes it from me, but I lay it down of my own accord. I have authority to lay it down and authority to take it up again. This command I received from my Father" (NIV). That text shows the cross to be the *ultimate act of obedience*, and it is not merely passive. His obedience to the Father consisted also in teaching in accordance with the Father's commands: "For I have not spoken on my own authority, but the Father who sent me has himself given me a commandment—what to say and what to speak" (12:49). Near the end of his earthly life, facing the onslaught of "the ruler of this world," Jesus says, "He has no claim on me, but I do as the Father has commanded me" (14:30–31).

Unlike the first Adam, Jesus will not be duped by Satan. On the night that he was betrayed, he prays to his Father and speaks of "having accomplished the work that you gave me to do" (17:4). The High Priestly Prayer in John 17 is filled with petitions based on the Son's accomplishment of the Father's will. More specifically, the accomplished work is the salvation of the people given to the Son by the Father. Jesus' obedience is the means to his being glorified as he was before the world began (v. 5) and to his followers' receiving eternal life (v. 2), being sanctified in the truth of God's word (v. 17), and entering into unity with the Son and the Father (vv. 21–23). The underlying theme in John 17 is, moreover, that the work accomplished by Jesus is not *ad hoc*, related only to his incarnation, but is the accomplishment of the

17. See also 5:30.

43

Father's plan before the creation of the world for the salvation of his people (vv. 2, 6, 8, 24).[18] Jesus' obedience is portrayed as one piece, both in life and in death, as the Son submits to his Father's will and carries out his will and commands, and so establishes the ground upon which "many will be made righteous." It is not a stretch to refer to this as a relationship of obliged and accepted obedience, a covenant.

Obedience Leads to Life. Second, the implied reward for Adam's obedience was life, just as obedience in the Mosaic covenant would be rewarded with life (e.g., Deut. 4:40; 5:33; 28:1–14). Life is also the reward gained by the Son for his obedience to the Father. The ultimate goal lost to disobedience is gained through the obedience of the second Adam. This idea is supported by the close connection between justification and life. Romans 5:12–21 is all about the contrast between death from Adam and life from Christ, and this on the basis of obedience and disobedience. The trespass of Adam and the free gift of God in Christ in verses 15–17 are ultimately what distinguish between death and life, for if death reigned through the sin of one man, then how "much more will those who receive the abundance of grace and the free gift of righteousness reign in life through the one man Jesus Christ?" (v. 17). Adam's trespass led to condemnation of the human race, but Christ's "one act of righteousness leads to justification and life for all men" (v. 18). That last phrase is best translated as "justification" (or "righteousness") "that *leads* to life."[19]

The justification that flows from Christ results in the ultimate reward of eternal life through the obedient second Adam. That Paul has the eschatological future in mind is clear from the distinct connection he makes just a few verses earlier between justification now and deliverance in the future.[20] In verse 9 he says, "We have now been justified by his blood, much more shall we be saved by him from the wrath of God." He follows that up by assuring his readers that if God reconciled his enemies

18. See Clark, "The Covenant before the Covenants," 192–94.
19. Moo, *Romans*, 341. See particularly n126.
20. Ibid. See also his discussion of 5:9–10, 309–12.

through Christ's death, "much more . . . shall we be saved by his life" (v. 10). The final verse in the chapter also orients us toward the future and again fuses justification and life: whereas "sin reigned in death," now, through Christ, grace reigns "through righteousness leading to eternal life through Jesus Christ our Lord" (v. 21).

1 Corinthians 15. In 1 Corinthians 15, the universal death of Adam is countered with the eternal life that flows from Christ: "For as in Adam all die, so also in Christ shall all be made alive" (v. 22).[21] Adam's sin brought a curse upon him, his children, and the earth, but Christ the second Adam defeated the curse so that those who bear the image of Adam would "bear the image of the man of heaven" (v. 49). The reason for bringing this text into the discussion at this point is to make another connection with the covenantal roles of Adam and Christ. First Corinthians 15 supports the representative relationship that Paul forges in Romans 5:12–22 between Adam and humanity and Christ and his people. Life is gained through Christ as death came through Adam: "For as by a man came death, by a man has come also the resurrection of the dead" (1 Cor. 15:21). As the "firstfruits" (v. 20), Christ's resurrection is representative of the future resurrection of God's people and marks the beginning of that end-time event in the present.[22] Although this text is not about obedience and disobedience, it does show powerfully that Christ as the second Adam secures what the first Adam lost, eternal life.

Romans 4:25. Another important text in this regard, and one linked to justification, is Romans 4:25, in which Paul says that Christ "was delivered up for our trespasses and raised for our justification." The justifying verdict of "righteous" comes only through the resurrection of Christ. The resurrection is not just the stamp of approval on Christ's work on the cross but

---

21. Richard Gaffin is right to call verse 22 "a virtual one-sentence summary of the teaching in Romans 5:12ff." *Resurrection and Redemption: A Study in Paul's Soteriology* (Phillipsburg, NJ: Presbyterian and Reformed, 1987), 36.

22. Ibid, 34–36.

is the inauguration of the new life and the new age to come.[23] As such, it vindicates the life and work of the second Adam who lived in obedience to the Father *and* died for the sins of Adam's children. In this way it is entirely correct to say that Christ himself was *justified*, that he was judged and declared to be legally in the right[24]—the proof being the reward of eternal life demonstrated at the resurrection. A similar point is made by Paul in 1 Timothy 3:16, where he speaks of Christ's being "manifested in the flesh" and "vindicated by the Spirit." The word in the ESV, "vindicated," could well be translated "declared" (or "proved") "to be right" (or "righteous").[25] Not only did Christ identify with sinners and become a sin offering on their behalf (cf. 2 Cor. 5:21), his resurrection also "identifies him with saints in the verdict of justification, which was given to him for his establishing of righteousness."[26] When God declares a sinner to be "just," it is on the basis of the verdict passed on the resurrected second Adam.

The twin issues of obedience and life give the relationship between the Father and Christ Jesus a distinct covenantal character. Whether one balks at the theological language, it is reasonable to say that (1) there was some sort of agreed plan carried out by Christ; (2) he carried out that plan by functioning in a subordinate role; (3) his obedience cannot be limited to so-called passive obedience but consisted of simultaneous submission and action; and (4) he fulfilled the role of second Adam through life-gaining obedience. The term "covenant of redemption" seems not so far-fetched after all. Now back to Romans 5.

23. A point made clear by Michael F. Bird in *Introducing Paul: The Man, His Mission and His Message* (Downers Grove, IL: IVP, 2008), particularly 76, 96, 166. Also see his *Saving Righteousness of God: Studies in Paul, Justification, and the New Perspective*, PBM (Milton Keynes, UK: Paternoster, 2007).
24. See G. K. Beale, "Resurrection in the Already-and-Not-Yet Phases of Justification," in *For the Fame of God's Name: Essays in Honor of John Piper*, ed. Sam Storms and Justin Taylor (Wheaton, IL: Crossway, 2010), 193–96.
25. Ibid. Beale cites this text as well, along with Rom. 4:25, Acts 17:31, Isa. 50:4–11, and Isa. 53.
26. Ibid., 196. At this point Beale is interacting with Richard Gaffin, *The Centrality of the Resurrection: A Study in Paul's Soteriology* (Grand Rapids: Baker, 1978), reprinted under the title *Resurrection and Redemption: A Study in Paul's Soteriology*.

From Sinners to Righteous

When Paul speaks of being "made" sinners and "will be made" righteous, he is speaking legally. He is not emphasizing, at least not here, either sinful or righteous actions. He is speaking of a status, a position that people occupy before God. Without doubt, actions accompany each status. Paul chronicles the sinfulness of the human race in Romans 1:18–3:20, and the ungodliness and sinfulness that characterizes humanity apart from Christ is more than evident (e.g., 3:23; 4:5; 5:6, 8). Likewise, in 4:18–21 Paul shows that Abraham's faith translated into his life, and in chapter 6 he heads off the accusation that his theology of justification leads to lawlessness by showing that the life of the justified is lived in service to righteousness (e.g., 6:13). But here, in 5:19, I believe that Paul is getting to the core of the matter, the most fundamental issue of human existence, namely, everyone's status before God according to whom they are connected, either to Adam or to Christ.

Made Righteous

The word "made" (*kathisthēmi*) is not strictly a synonym for "impute" (*logizomai*).[27] Imputation language, as found in 4:1–8, 22, is not the language of 5:19. It is worth noting that faith, so central in Romans 4 in connection with imputation, is not highlighted here either. In Romans 3 and 4 Paul established both the necessity of justification by faith and imputation as the way in which God grants us a righteous standing. Here he provides the basis for justification by faith and the source of the righteousness counted to the believer by faith, just as he accounts for the source by which people "were made sinners." In the New Testament, the same word translated as "made" in 5:19 is most commonly used to designate the place and/or status a thing or person holds or to which a thing or a person is appointed.[28] Less commonly the

27. A fairly detailed study of the Greek word *kathisthēmi* can be found in *Jesus' Blood and Righteousness*, 115–22; although at the time I was a bit too uncritical of some of the data I used in that study, I still hold to the conclusions that I reached.
28. See Matt. 25:21, 23; Luke 12:14; Acts 6:3; Titus 1:5; Heb. 5:1.

JUSTIFICATION BY GRACE THROUGH FAITH

word carries the sense of *become, cause to be,* or *make* and refers to some state of being.[29] Neither New Testament writers, nor those who translated the Old Testament into Greek, use it as a synonym for *impute.* But something of a dilemma arises here. Although it is true that if words are allowed to mean everything, they wind up meaning nothing, being too rigid when dealing with the meaning of words, not just in one language but in two (in this case Greek and English), can create false distinctions. This is particularly true when considering the matter of context.

In 5:19 the phrase "will be made righteous" refers to being put into a position, like the way we sometimes use the word *appoint,* as in "he was *appointed* to be federal judge." But the position (whether sinner or righteous) cannot be separated from the source of the position. First, Paul established the imputation of righteousness through faith in chapter 4. Second, it is clear from 5:18–19 that the legal status that one has before God is on the basis of *someone else's* actions. People are recognized in connection to Adam as those who sinned and in connection to Christ as those who fulfilled everything needed to be deemed righteous.[30] The status with which we are appointed is due to the fact that we are counted to have sinned in Adam and counted to have obeyed in Christ. So while *made* does not mean *impute,* the two are inseparable actions.[31] This is why even though *impute* is not used here, Romans 5:12–21 is historically associated with the imputation of sin and righteousness.

It is the meaning of *made* that helps in the interpretation of what it means to be a sinner or righteous. Typically, in the New Testament the word translated *righteous* in 5:19 describes behavior

---

29. See James 4:4, "*makes* himself an enemy of God," and 2 Peter 1:8, "If these [qualities] are yours . . . they *keep you from being* ineffective or unfruitful."

30. The distinction can be important because, as Piper says, we are not just given Adam's status: "We are counted as having *sinned* in Adam" (his emphasis). Similarly, it is not just "Christ's *status*" that becomes ours: "Rather, in Christ we are counted as having done all the righteousness God requires." John Piper, *The Future of Justification: A Response to N. T. Wright* (Wheaton, IL: Crossway, 2007), 170–71. Even so, it is impossible not to use the word *status* at certain points when speaking of our legal position before God.

31. In addition, Paul has already established righteousness through imputation in Romans 4, and that provides the backdrop for understanding what is at work when a person is "made" righteous.

and/or personal character. For example, Joseph (Matt. 1:19), Simeon (Luke 2:25), Joseph of Arimathea (Luke 23:50), and Cornelius (Acts 10:22) are all referred to as righteous.[32] Paul uses the word in this way as well (Rom. 3:10; Col. 4:1; Titus 1:8; 2 Tim. 4:8). So, the word denotes righteous acts or describes a person's character, but when he pairs it with *made*, which refers to being appointed or placed into a position, then *righteous* is not focused on behavior or character but on our position before God. We are made to hold the position of those whose acts and behavior are righteous on the basis of Christ's obedience. This does not amount to a different meaning of the word *righteous*—it basically means what it usually means. It is just that here Paul asserts that what is typically recognized through character traits and/or actions is declared *apart from* any actions done on the part of those made righteous. Of course, God creates what he declares, and those "made righteous" are fully expected to show that God is not a liar, but it is possible and vitally necessary to distinguish the basis from the result, or more plainly, the root from the fruit. The basis of righteousness here is the obedience of Jesus, and to mix in the transformed life of the believer misses Paul's fundamental point.[33] The pairing *righteous* with *made*, according to the way it's defined here, is nothing short of staggering: through the obedience of Christ, God judges those connected (by faith) to Christ, who own him as their covenant head, as *having fully accomplished all manner of righteousness in his eyes*. If we grasp the depth of our connection to Christ, then we will understand that what is his, namely life and righteousness, is ours.

Conclusion: Christ-Centered Justification

When we hear the word *justification*, our thoughts should not go first to things like the role of faith and works, justification

---

32. Among other examples in the Gospels and Acts are Matt. 10:41; 23:35; Mark 6:20; Luke 1:6; 18:9; Acts 3:14; 7:52 (both in reference to Christ).

33. "The forensic and the transformative are not merged together here, but we do see that the legal is the basis of the transformative." Thomas R. Schreiner, *Paul: Apostle of God's Glory in Christ: A Pauline Theology* (Downers Grove, IL: IVP, 2001), 209.

in an order of salvation, the eschatological nature of justification, or much less whether we are up to speed on all the latest discussions and debates. All these things are important, but we must remember that the prior issue is what Christ has done *for us* in his life and death. Totally apart from our faith, works, and knowledge, the foundation for our righteousness was achieved by and resides in the second and true Adam. These are not just noble and eternal truths meant only for musing over or discussing with a few interested people; they are the very core of what we proclaim in the larger story of the gospel.

With the triumphal obedience of the last Adam established, it is now time to turn back to the pages of Genesis and meet again our father in the faith, if not in the flesh. It is through the story of Abraham that we encounter the first explicit mention of faith in the Bible, and it is here that we learn how the righteousness that God supplies becomes ours, and also where we find the beginnings of the biblical discussion of what it looks like to be those justified by God.

3

Not by Sight: Abraham and the Righteousness of Faith

THE NEXT TWO CHAPTERS deal largely with how God counts righteousness to people by faith. In the story of Abraham, two of the main building blocks for the biblical doctrine of justification appear together—faith and righteousness. We are also introduced to the fundamental concept of imputation. First we will consider the narrative of Abraham in the Old Testament, while the next chapter looks at Abraham in Paul's letters. Here is a road map.

- Abraham in Context
- God Speaks
- Righteousness of Faith
- God's Covenant: Future Promises on Past Evidence
- Life in the Covenant
- The Righteous Live by Faith
- Confirming the Promises
- Conclusion

Abraham in Context

We first meet Abraham in a world of confusion. For the most part, Genesis 3:7–11:9 is a downward spiral of fits and starts, each

51

ending in failure. Yet the story does continue, and rays of hope shine through the darkness. Subtly the narrative teaches something vital for understanding the entire message of the Bible— hope for the human race must come from outside. In order to see the significance of Abraham and what his story teaches, particularly the magnitude of what God does in and through him, we need briefly to recap the history leading to him.[1]

The Wrath of God Revealed

Although they are outside the garden and under God's curse, Adam and Eve nevertheless have children. But if there is any doubt that things are not as they ought to be, their firstborn son Cain gathers plants grown by his own hand as a sacrifice to God. His brother Abel sacrifices an animal. God accepts Abel's blood sacrifice offered in faith (Heb. 11:4) but rejects Cain's offering. Overwhelmed with jealousy, Cain kills his younger brother. Cain did at least try to cover up his sin, knowing the guilt and shame that his parents felt when they disobeyed. A few generations later, however, one of Cain's descendants, Lamech, kills a young man and writes a song about it.[2] Shame, known in the garden and by the first murderer, is now glory.

The creation mandate to have children is carried out after the fall, but as more people appear, that which was meant for good (filling the world with people) becomes a malevolent force. As the human race increases, so does the flow of sin into the world. Wickedness and evil are met by God's grief and judgment (6:6–7). As final judgment looms, Noah appears.

1. The first eleven chapters of Genesis are not only crucial for understanding faith and righteousness in the story of Abraham but are also, as Dumbrell points out, "critical for the development of a biblical world view and thus a biblical theology." William J. Dumbrell, *The Faith of Israel: Its Expression in the Books of the Old Testament* (Grand Rapids: Baker, 1988), 23.

2. Dempster well describes the genealogy from Cain ("the brother killer") to Lamech ("the child-killer") in 4:17–24: "In a few verses the writer is able to convey a sense of the catastrophic descent of the human race from covering up killing to boasting in bloodletting." Stephen G. Dempster, *Dominion and Dynasty: A Theology of the Hebrew Bible* (Downers Grove, IL: IVP, 2001), 70.

Saved but Not Improved

God saves Noah, his family, and pairs of animals from his judgment of the flood. When the water subsides, an Eden-like scene unfolds as the human race and the animal kingdom emerge from the chaos of the flood—similar to the way they first appeared when God created the world out of the void. The creation mandate is reiterated: "Be fruitful and multiply and fill the earth" (9:1). Noah and his children are presented as stewards over the earth, and God gives them both animals and plants for food. God displays his grace in making a covenant with the world: he will never again destroy the world with water, and as a guarantee he leaves a sign in the sky as a reminder of his promise. But as the saying goes, "You can't go home again," at least not yet.[3]

The scene after the flood is not, as it is sometimes characterized, exactly a renewal of Eden. To be sure, God's grace and kindness are on display, and there are obvious parallels in themes and words, but God does not start over from scratch with Noah. God begins where things left off, and it soon becomes clear that the situation has not improved. For one, God states plainly that "the intention of man's heart is evil from his youth" (8:21) even while promising not to bring destruction on the world in a similar way again. It is also clear from events in the story. For instance, in the post-flood world murder is expressly prohibited, but the very prohibition signals that the problem is still there. There will be more Cains, but now there is a specific law by which to judge them, making sin all the more sinful. Things are not, to say the least, the way they ought to be.

Bloodlines of Promise

From the midst of the narrative a promise arises that will reverberate through the rest of the Bible, although at times only through genealogies. Noah's son Shem will gain ascendancy, God will bless Japheth by allowing him a place with Shem, and the

3. In reality, we will never go back to Adam's first home. Later we find out that Eden was just an image of what is to come.

Canaanites, descents of Ham, will serve them both. Ultimately, Shem's line will lead to the fulfillment of the promise that the descendants of the Serpent will be crushed by a descendant of Eve (3:15), and that story begins to unfold at this point in Genesis. But it has to wait for the account of yet another debacle by the children of Adam. The builders of the tower of Babel were motivated by one basic desire, to establish themselves on their own terms, on the basis of their own works, apart from God.[4] God will have nothing of the sort, so he does something to check their shameless self-promotion—he confuses the languages, which leads to the division of the human race into the nations. Then, just when things look the bleakest, two genealogies appear one verse after the Babel incident: those of Shem and his descendant Terah, father of Abram.

When we read biblical genealogies carefully, we often find that besides being records of God's faithfulness, they contain vital pieces of very specific information, and none more so than Terah's genealogy in 11:30. The wives of all three of Terah's sons are named, but there is a particular detail given about Abram's wife, Sarai: she cannot have children. For all intents and purposes, Abram's part in the story seems to end as quickly as it begins. He was Terah's son; he married Sarai; she was barren; the end. This sets the stage for chapter 12 and makes the upcoming events all the more astounding.

The reason it is important to take the time to recount the events of Genesis 3–11 is that these chapters contain an account of abject human failure and divine judgment, ending with a couple living without hope and without God in the world. By the time the narrative gets to chapter 12, it is more than evident that human beings are unable to right what happened in Eden. At the same time, another pattern is established during the account of the first

4. Dumbrell suggests (rightly) that what God punished "was the problem of the misplaced center." He goes on to explain what this means: "Human beings regarded themselves as the measure of all things, able to control the course of their world, able to build better worlds! Of course, by such an endeavor the naked meaning of sin is exposed. Such human attempts, then and since, which leave God out of consideration are sin in its baldest and most blatant form." *The Faith of Israel*, 23.

centuries of our history. God, although he decisively condemns and judges sin, does not give up on mankind or the creation, in spite of the increasing distance they have put between themselves and God. The narrative of Genesis 3–11 and its themes of failure and judgment prepare the way for the story of Abraham and the declaration of righteousness. The narrative sets up the Abraham story, just as Romans 1:18–3:20, an extended discussion of sin and God's judgment that follows the presentation of justification in 1:16–17, prepares for Paul's discussion of righteousness and justification in 3:21–5:21. The phrase "Now the LORD said to Abram" that begins Genesis 12:1 works in the narrative similar to the way "But now the righteousness of God has been manifested" (Rom. 3:21) works in Paul's letter. Reading Genesis 12 without chapters 3–11 is like reading Romans 3:21 and what follows apart from what Paul says earlier. Against the dark background of human failure and the resulting judgment, God's grace takes center stage.

God Speaks

While the first eleven chapters of Genesis cover centuries, the next ten chapters cover one generation.[5] The narrative slows down to record how God's plan of redemption unfolds. At the end of chapter 11, Abraham moves his family from Ur to Haran, and it is at Haran that the Lord speaks to him and makes a promise.[6] The Lord will bless Abraham, he will become a great nation, and all the nations of the earth will be blessed through him. God also pledges to pay special attention to Abraham, promising to be on his side and protect him: "I will bless those who bless you, and him who dishonors you I will curse" (12:3).

Who is Abraham that he should be the recipient of such a great promise? He is from a region (Ur of the Chaldeans, later known as Babylon) that Scripture usually associates with evil and idolatry, but beyond that we have no other specific biographical

5. Dempster, *Dominion and Dynasty*, 76.
6. Of course at this point he is "Abram," but I will use "Abraham" throughout.

information about him except the important fact that he stands in the line of Shem. But even with his lineage there is still no indication in the text that he was any more worthy than his brothers Nahor and Haran. Someone might suppose that there was *something* about Abraham that caused the Lord to call him, but remember that up to this point in the Bible there are individuals whose character and/or behavior get special notice. We know that "Enoch walked with God" (5:22) and that "Noah found favor in the eyes of the LORD" and "was a righteous man, blameless in his generation" (6:8–9). Of Abraham, however, there is no such comment. Even after the Lord calls Abraham, it is apparent from his behavior, particularly his tendencies when powerful men are around his beautiful wife (12:11–20; 20:1–18), that he is far from perfect. Abraham's only claim is that the Lord chose to call him from the line of Shem and bring him into a special relationship through which the Lord would save the world.

Hope in What Is Not Seen

Even a casual reader will notice a snag in the plan. A vital ingredient needed to make someone a "great nation" is missing—Sarah cannot get pregnant. On top of that, we are told that Abraham is advancing in years, being already seventy-five when he left Haran (12:4). These things, along with the trajectory of sin and failure traced earlier, leave us to draw the conclusion that hope for the fulfillment of the promise will have to come from somewhere unseen.

As Abraham's story continues, something of a pattern develops: Abraham follows God's leading and God continues to show himself true to his word. Abraham responds to God's word and promise by building an altar to worship the Lord (12:8). He wavers in Egypt, fearing that Pharaoh's desire for Sarah may prove fatal to him (vv. 11–13), and ends up making a profit (v. 16); nevertheless, God acts on Sarah's behalf and strikes Pharaoh with plagues (v. 17). Afterward he returns to where he built the first altar and again worships God (13:4). Later he divides the land between himself and Lot, allowing Lot to choose the Jordan valley while he takes Canaan. Here the Lord appears to Abraham and tells him to look every direction because his descendants, who will be greater in number than the dust of the earth, will inherit this land (vv. 14–17). He defeats four kings, saves his nephew Lot, and receives a blessing from the priest-king Melchizedek, refusing to take his share of the spoils of war because of an oath he swore to the Lord (14:22–24). Abraham is walking with God, and more importantly God is clearly on Abraham's side—there is an implicit relationship between them, and this relationship will soon be affirmed. The promise, however, remains unfulfilled.

Righteousness Reckoned through Faith

Years later, just when Abraham is prepared to take matters into his own hands and make Eliezer, a member of his household, his heir, God again steps in with a word of promise: "Fear not, Abram, I am your shield; your reward shall be very great" (15:1). This time God will seal his promise with a solemn, unbreakable oath.

Abraham's decision to make Eliezer his heir is not exactly a highlight-reel moment of faith. The reader can sympathize—it has been years since God promised him a great nation, but he still does not have a child. According to what he can see around him, there is no hope except Eliezer.[7] Abraham's frustration is heard in his words to God: "You have given me no children; so a servant in my household will be my heir" (v. 3, NIV). God, however, has his own plan:

> Then the word of the LORD came to him: "This man will not be your heir, but a son who is your own flesh and blood will be your heir." He took him outside and said, "Look up at the heavens and count the stars—if indeed you can count them." Then he said to him, "So shall your offspring be." (vv. 4–5, NIV)

7. Bruce Waltke, *An Old Testament Theology* (Grand Rapids: Zondervan, 2007), 333.

Then, for the first time in the Bible, an extremely important word appears: "And he *believed* the LORD, and he counted it to him as righteousness" (v. 6). Clearly this is not the first time that faith is exercised in the biblical narrative. Just imagine what it took for Noah to build an ark. Verse 6 is not the first time that Abraham believes, either. If the narrative of Genesis is not enough to establish it, then there is the definite word in Hebrews: "By faith Abraham obeyed when he was called to go out to a place that he was to receive as an inheritance. And he went out, not knowing where he was going" (Heb. 11:8). Why, then, does the word *believed* appear for the first time here? The best answer is that it is tied directly to righteousness before God. Abraham's belief in God's promise amounts to righteousness in the eyes of God.

Righteousness of Faith

Typically the word *righteousness* is associated with what a person does or how a person and/or his actions are characterized. When Abraham's faith in the Lord is counted to him as righteousness, it means that God sees Abraham as someone who has fulfilled his (God's) standard of what it means to be righteous. He is deemed a righteous person. Here, however, it is not Abraham's behavior or actions that constitute his righteousness but his faith in God.[8] That is an important point to make—it is not faith in the abstract that is counted as righteousness but specifically faith in the Lord God. Abraham is not what is often referred to these days as a "man of faith." His faith cannot be separated from its object, God and his word of promise. Abraham believes *God*. Because Abraham believes the promise for an heir, God counts Abraham as holding the same status or position as that of a person who has done everything

---

8. As this is not the beginning of Abraham's faith, we can assume it is not the point at which he is justified. It was justifying faith that brought him out of Ur. In the text, however, justifying faith is made explicit at the moment of Abraham's crises of trying to live by faith. This is a narrative, not an epistle, so it teaches us in different ways.

right according to God's standards.[9] This way of understanding this text is not based simply on what the word *righteousness* *can* mean (although obviously important) but what it means when paired with the word *counted* and when what is counted is faith in God.

Counted as Righteousness

There are basically two ways that a thing or a person can be "counted" as something. First, a thing can be *counted*, we might say *recognized*, as being what it is. Over time a man's integrity, honesty, and overall pleasing disposition might earn him the distinguished title a "good guy." People call someone a "good guy" because they have seen the evidence in his life and in their dealings with him. According to our standards, a man is a "good guy" because it is truly the case. A biblical example of this sort of counting is found in the description of Phinehas in Psalm 106:30–31.[10] In the era to which the psalmist refers (see Num. 25), many Israelite men had developed a taste for Moabite women and their gods, specifically Baal of Peor. At the Lord's command, Moses orders the judges to kill any men who had fallen into this idolatry. The next thing that happens, an Israelite man saunters up to the Tent of Meeting with a Midianite woman. Phinehas jumps up, grabs a spear, and kills them both. The psalmist declares that Phinehas's act was "counted to him as righteousness." In the midst of personal and national sin, Phinehas steps up and acts on behalf of the Lord and in accordance with the covenant. Over against the unfaithfulness of Israel (which the psalmist recounts in detail), Phinehas's action is recognized for what it is, a righteous act.

9. "Abraham places his entire trust in the prophetic word that promises, as it were, the birth of an heir from the dead. . . . God reckons his faith in the seed, pregnant with its fulfillment in Jesus Christ, equivalent to meeting his moral demands." Waltke, *An Old Testament Theology*, 334.

10. See D. A. Carson, "The Vindication of Imputation: On Fields of Discourse and Semantic Fields," in *Justification: What's at Stake in the Current Debates*, ed. Mark Husbands and Daniel J. Treier (Downers Grove, IL: IVP, 2004); in regard to Phinehas, see particularly page 57. I discuss this issue in some detail in *Jesus' Blood and Righteousness: Paul's Theology of Imputation* (Wheaton, IL: Crossway, 2006), 80–83, 86–88.

On the other hand, a thing may be counted to be something it is not by nature. I have a small, olive green New Testament that in terms of market value may be worth a few dollars. It is the New Testament given to my father on the eve of D-Day and which he carried with him all across France and Belgium. As a book, even as an Army issue from World War II, it is not worth much, but I count that book as priceless. Is it "priceless"? On one level it is not. But I view it as one of the most valuable things I have, counting it of more value than many things I own that are worth far more money. In that way, you can say that I count the book as something it is not. The Bible contains such examples of counting also. Consider Proverbs 27:14: "Whoever blesses his neighbor with a loud voice, rising early in the morning, will be counted as cursing." A blessing is not cursing; in fact it is just the opposite. But in the right context, a blessing—coming from a loud and likely pious and zealous neighbor early in the morning—might as well be cursing.[11] The blessing is counted to be something it is not.

The counting of Abraham's faith as righteousness fits in the second category. Faith is not counted as righteousness in the same way that Phinehas' righteous act is counted as righteousness. It is not something that Abraham does or intends to do. Take into consideration that the moment of counting occurs right when Abraham was intending to fulfill God's promise himself. But Abraham believes what the Lord says to him; he takes the Lord at his word and trusts him to do what he promises. The status or description typically reserved for actions is here counted to Abraham on the basis of faith. Abraham's faith is counted to him as something it inherently is not, righteousness. Reading the words together this way means that it is not simply because one can find examples of *righteousness* used in a forensic or legal sense in the Old Testament, but because when paired with *counted* and *faith*, righteousness here refers to a judgment and declaration about Abraham's position before God. What might usually be declared

11. See Carson, "The Vindication of Imputation," 58.

over a person who did what is right in God's sight is declared upon Abraham through faith.

God's Covenant: Future Promises on Past Evidence

Three things follow the declaration of righteousness. First, God states who he is and what he has done for Abraham in the past. He says to Abraham, "I am the LORD who brought you out from Ur of the Chaldeans to give you this land to possess" (Gen. 15:7). Whatever God has or will promise Abraham for the future is grounded in God's action in the past. It is worth noting that this statement comes just one verse after the first mention of Abraham's faith; this marks the basic pattern of faith expressed in the rest of the Bible. Biblical faith in God and his promises is hope for the future based on God's work in the past that transforms life in the present. Faith is always an intersection of past, present, and future.

Second, God declares what he is going to do for Abraham:

> Know for certain that your offspring will be sojourners in a land that is not theirs and will be servants there, and they will be afflicted for four hundred years. But I will bring judgment on the nation that they serve, and afterward they shall come out with great possessions. As for you, you shall go to your fathers in peace; you shall be buried in a good old age. (vv. 13–15)

God assures Abraham that he is going to keep his word and shows Abraham a specific future for his family and for him. Abraham will have a family, and their future is already established by God before a child is born. God also shows Abraham the end of his own life—a life that ends in peace, protected and blessed by God.

Third, God binds himself to his word: "When the sun had gone down and it was dark, behold, a smoking fire pot and a flaming torch passed between these pieces" (v. 17). These three things confirm the relationship between God and Abraham, a covenant: "On that day the LORD made a covenant with Abram" (v. 18).

There are many striking features in this text, but none more so than the fact that God initiates, establishes, and seals the covenant with Abraham. Abraham is of course a part of this relationship and must fulfill his covenant role in particular ways (as we will see shortly), but the establishment of the covenant itself is not conditioned on Abraham's performance; it is a gift of God's grace. This should not come as a surprise to anyone familiar with the story up to this point. The track record of the human race from Genesis 3 to 11 hardly suggests a two-way street between God and man. God is not reacting to human efforts or cries for help. No one is reaching up to God; God is acting on his own initiative according to his own will and pleasure. If the chasm between God and humanity is going to be spanned, then it must be God who builds the bridge. This is the way it always is with God and man. No one meets God halfway, or takes even one baby step toward him—God meets us in our sin, as we are under his curse and doomed to death.

An Unbreakable Oath

The events taking place in Genesis 15 can be quite strange to many modern readers, although to others who have heard it explained so many times it can become commonplace. It is crucial to understand what happens here, and for those already familiar with the text it is just as crucial not to become so familiar with it that the graphic and stunning message is lost. The dramatic event is introduced with a question—Abraham is asking for assurance that God will indeed give him the land: "O Lord GOD, how am I to know that I shall possess it?" (v. 8). God does not respond with "Because I said so," which might be enough coming from God. God intends to make it clear to Abraham that not only does he mean what he says, but he will obligate himself to do it.

What follows is an elaborate and extraordinarily messy business of a cow, a goat, and a ram split in two and laid side by side with two birds (vv. 9–10). When this is done, Abraham falls into a deep sleep surrounded by "dreadful and great darkness" (v. 12), tipping off the reader that something unworldly is about to happen. And it does. God again gives Abraham a very particular word about his future family—after four hundred years of living and suffering in a different land, they will return and Canaan will be theirs (vv. 13–16)—and then: "When the sun had gone down and it was dark, behold, a smoking fire pot and a flaming torch passed between these pieces" (v. 17). This is a page taken out of ancient Near Eastern practice. First, God has already promised to protect Abraham, the very thing a powerful king would promise when entering into covenant relationship with a lesser ruler. Second, when a covenant was made between two kings, they would cut animals in two and walk between them as a sign of an oath, basically saying, "If I break this covenant, then let me die like one of these animals." The really amazing thing here is that it is not two kings, or even God and Abraham together, but only God who passes between the gore.[12] God takes upon himself a binding oath to fulfill the promises of this covenant. This is a covenant of grace sealed by God, and through it God will enact his purpose to save the human race.

Life in the Covenant

Sometimes God's covenant with Abraham is called *unconditional*. God declares Abraham's faith in him as righteousness and takes the burden of fulfilling his promise on himself. Abraham's future is guaranteed by God. However, the word *unconditional* might suggest that since Abraham is counted righteous by faith and God has sealed his promise, Abraham (and subsequently his children) has no real responsibility for his side of the relationship. If that is what is meant by *unconditional*, then it does not match the teaching of the Bible. Sometimes it is easy to give the impression that, yes, obedience is important, but at the end of

12. The smoke and flame are surely signs of the presence of God, calling to mind images like the burning bush on Horeb (Ex. 3:2) and the cloud and the fire that led Israel through the wilderness (13:21–22). ·

the day it does not matter all that much, except perhaps for getting rewards. Again, this is not the way that the Bible puts things. The best way to think of it is to say that God unconditionally initiates and guarantees the covenant, but the relationship is not just one-sided; there is an expectation that Abraham and his descendants will live within the bounds established by God for the relationship.[13] The emphasis in this covenant is on what God promises to do, but Abraham's side of the covenant is very much in the picture too.

Consider what God says when he establishes circumcision as a covenantal sign in chapter 17. God says to Abraham: "I am God Almighty; walk before me, and be blameless, that I may make my covenant between me and you, and may multiply you greatly" (vv. 1–2). The reader may again feel the tension. This is the same God who bound himself to keep his word to Abraham, and now he is commanding Abraham to live in obedience. Here is how it appears in the text.

God's *I Wills*:
v. 4: You shall be the father of a multitude of nations (God's work).
v. 5: I have made you the father of many nations.
v. 6: I will make you exceedingly fruitful and make you into nations.
v. 7: I will establish my covenant between me and you and your offspring . . . for an everlasting covenant to be God to you and your offspring.
v. 8: I will give you and your offspring . . . all the land of Canaan for an everlasting possession, and I will be their God.

These verses are filled with *I will* statements from God and promises for a future that seem certain. The other side of the coin is God's commands and warnings to Abraham.

13. As Fesko puts it, "Though emphasis lies upon the unilateral administration of this (the Abrahamic) covenant, the bilateral element is present in the expected response (Gen. 17:1, 9–14)." J. V. Fesko, *Justification: Understanding the Classic Reformed Doctrine* (Phillipsburg, NJ: P&R Publishing, 2008), 111.

You Will:

v. 9: You shall keep my covenant, you and your offspring after you.

v. 10: Every male among you shall be circumcised.

v. 14: Any uncircumcised male . . . shall be cut off from his people; he has broken my covenant.

God is going to keep his word, but Abraham and his children must show themselves to be God's people. It appears that for Abraham and his children, obedience is a necessary part of gaining the inheritance that God promises. This is not the only place where this tension surfaces. To the contrary, it increases.

"Since" or "So That"—Which Is It?

In chapter 18 heavenly visitors come and announce that in one year Sarah will have a son. Then, along with Abraham, they set out to have a look at Sodom. On the way the Lord speaks, and what he says usually goes unnoticed in discussions about justification. It is good to read it slowly and pay careful attention to specific words:

> The LORD said, "Shall I hide from Abraham what I am about to do, *seeing that* Abraham shall *surely* become a great and mighty nation, and all the nations of the earth *shall* be blessed in him? For I have *chosen* him, *that* he may command his children and his household after him *to keep* the way of the LORD *by doing* righteousness and justice, *so that* the LORD may bring to Abraham what he has promised him. (18:17–19)

The answer to the question "Shall I hide . . . ?" is clearly "no," and the reason is clear: since Abraham is going to inherit the promise, God will not keep him in the dark about what is going to happen at Sodom. Why will Abraham inherit the promise? Because God chose him. This all fits well with the discussion of chapters 12 and 15. Then comes the other part: Abraham was chosen for a purpose, to teach his children to obey the Lord. Then we find out exactly how obedience to the Lord is done: "by doing righteousness and justice." This is a good example of *righteousness* (the same word used before) as something that is *done*, and here it is matched with justice.[14] Then follows the most surprising thing of all: Abraham, chosen by God and promised a great nation, will teach his children to obey the Lord *so that* the Lord will do as he promised! Two distinct things are said here. According to verses 17–18, the promise is in the bank. God is going to do exactly as he said. According to verse 19, God will do as he said if Abraham's children live in obedience.

It is entirely right to say that God will keep his promise unconditionally to Abraham. At no point does God rescind his word or add caveats that provide ways to amend or back out of his promise. Chapters 17 and 18 do not contradict chapters 12 and 15. God freely called Abraham by his own initiative, declared Abraham's faith in him as righteousness, and confirmed his covenant relationship with him, sealing it with an oath. The condition for the fulfillment of the promise is on the part of the one who pledged to keep it, who is God. Later on in Abraham's life we see the initial evidence that God keeps his word with the birth of Isaac in chapter 21.

At the same time the blessing is unconditionally promised to a particular sort of people. What we learn in chapters 17 and 18 (and later 22) is that the children of the promise, the people of God, are a special people. The people of God must live in obedience to him and do what he commands and desires of them.[15] To state it negatively and in the context of Abraham, the children of

14. The dual obedience of righteousness and justice will appear prominently in the Mosaic covenant.

15. This is precisely how it is put to the children of Abraham several centuries later: "And Joshua said to all the people, 'Thus says the LORD, the God of Israel, "Long ago, your fathers lived beyond the Euphrates, Terah, the father of Abraham and of Nahor; and they served other gods"'" (Josh. 24:2). Then, after rehearsing God's faithfulness to them beginning with Abraham down to the present, he says: "Now therefore fear the LORD and serve him in sincerity and in faithfulness. Put away the gods that your fathers served beyond the River and in Egypt, and serve the LORD" (v. 14). This text also speaks to what Abraham was doing before God called him.

the promise cannot go back to Ur and serve idols as their fathers did and at the same time expect God to say, "I will be their God." Obedience, doing "justice and righteousness," is a necessary part of being the people of God. This idea will continue through the Mosaic covenant, where obedience will receive special emphasis, and ultimately into the new covenant, in which people of whom God says "I will be their God, and they shall be my people" (Jer. 31:33) will obey God from the heart. Ultimately what we see is that God will create the kind of people he wants by giving them his Spirit. So Genesis 17 and 18 are pointing forward to what God is going to do to fulfill his promise—establish a covenant in which people will obey him from the heart, a heart given by him. God provides the condition for fulfilling the unconditional covenant.

Reading the story of Abraham this way interprets it entirely in the context of promise and fulfillment. Chapter 15 begins to establish that faith is *the* way of relating to and being accepted by God. Genesis 17 and 18 begin to establish that faith is evidenced through obedience. I say *begin* because there are still many chapters of redemption that have to unfold before the whole story is put together in the Bible. Knowing the whole story as we do, however, we can see here in Genesis the historical contours of what is worked out later in both Old and New Testaments. There is a well-known example in the story of Abraham that illustrates the life of the justified. Centuries later, James will cite this story to argue against justification by dead faith.

The Righteous Live by Faith

Many sermons on Genesis 22 stress the emotional anguish and dread that Abraham undoubtedly felt as he went to sacrifice Isaac. It typically goes something like this.

> Just imagine: Abraham waited twenty-five years for a child. Finally, after waiting all that time, Isaac was born. All his hopes and dreams rested on that boy. Then, out of the blue, the unthinkable happens. God comes and tells Abraham that he has to sacrifice his

beloved son, Isaac. Abraham goes out in the morning, unable to look at Isaac, tears welling up in his eyes not just at the thought of losing his son but of killing him! As he walks up the mountain, his feet are like lead as every step brings him closer and closer to something more horrifying than anything a parent can imagine. Then, trembling, he ties his beloved son to the altar, stares into Isaac's eyes, raises the knife, and . . . .

It is not difficult to understand why we think these sorts of things when we hear the story of Abraham and Isaac. I believe that we are meant to feel the weight of the story. A nation was promised to a barren couple who finally have a child, and then God asks for the life of the child. Then there is the undeniable sympathy we feel for Abraham as we imagine what he experienced that day. Even though the story is resolved at the end, there is no way to avoid the inevitable thoughts and feelings it provokes in us. However, reading the text through experience—Abraham's or ours—does not capture the whole story. We have to read the clear emotional aspect of the story *along with* what is emphasized in the text. When we do, what we will find is that the story is not simply about how Abraham felt but the obedience of his faith.

If ever a story showed what it means to live by faith rather than sight, this one does. God comes to Abraham and commands: "Take your son, your only son Isaac, whom you love, and go to the land of Moriah, and offer him there as a burnt offering on one of the mountains of which I shall tell you" (v. 2). Here is how Abraham responds.

The Response of Faith

- Wakes up early, gets supplies, and sets out
- Tells his servants that he and Isaac will return from the mountain
- Takes wood and a knife and goes with Isaac up the mountain
- Tells Isaac that God will provide a sacrifice
- Builds an altar, ties up Isaac, and places him on it
- Reaches for his knife

In spite of the intense inner turmoil that Abraham must have experienced, he did not waiver in unbelief but trusted God to keep his promise and so persevered in obedience.[16] As seen earlier with Adam in Genesis 2, this is a test of Abraham's faith. Perhaps it might also be called a test of Abraham's responsibility to his covenantal relationship with God. Whatever the test is called, God declares that Abraham passed: "Do not lay your hand on the boy or do anything to him, for now I know that you fear God, seeing you have not withheld your son, your only son, from me" (Gen. 22:12). Then, in the wake of obedience, God reaffirms that he will keep his promises.

> By myself I have sworn, declares the LORD, because you have done this and have not withheld your son, your only son, I will surely bless you, and I will surely multiply your offspring as the stars of heaven and as the sand that is on the seashore. And your offspring shall possess the gate of his enemies, and in your offspring shall all the nations of the earth be blessed, because you have obeyed my voice. (vv. 16–18)

The language of verses 16–18 is taken right from the earlier promises:

Confirming the Promises

- "I will surely bless you" = "I will bless you and make your name great" (12:2).
- "As the stars of heaven" = "the stars . . . so shall your off-spring be" (15:5).
- "All the nations . . . blessed" = "all the families of the earth shall be blessed" (12:3).

In addition, the sand on the shore is quite similar to the pledge God made when the land was divided between Abraham and Lot: "I will make your offspring as the dust of the earth" (13:16),

16. Alluding to Rom. 4:18–21.

and the promise that his offspring will "possess the gate of his enemies" likely finds a parallel in 15:18–21, where Abraham's children are promised the land of the Canaanite nations. Moriah confirms these promises.

The promise(s) were at no point up in the air. God swore to keep his word to Abraham, his children, and the nations, but he wills to keep it through people whose faith in him is displayed in obedience. Of course God *knew* that Abraham feared him, but what happens on the mountain with Isaac is an open display of Abraham's faith—a faith that works—and an affirmation that God's declaration of righteousness in chapter 15 is true. God speaks the truth and declares what is right.

Conclusion

The story of Abraham does not solve the chaos of Genesis 3–11, but it points the way to how God is going to set things right. God is going to deal with the world through the children of Abraham, ultimately through a particular child, the seed that fulfills the promise (Gal. 3:14). It also establishes that people are not righteous before God on the basis of what they do but by faith. Abraham's faith sets the pattern for the rest of the Bible as a faith that believes God in spite of all visual evidence that may point to the contrary. Long before the law appears, it is well established that righteousness before God comes only by faith. However, while Abraham sets the standard for justification by faith alone, he also proves the old Protestant phrase, "we are justified by faith alone, but the faith that justifies is never alone." Abraham's faith is demonstrated as true faith through his obedience. The relationship between faith and righteousness and between faith and obedience is hammered out in the narrative of Abraham's life. For that reason it is not difficult to see why he is the key Old Testament figure in Paul's theology of justification. Abraham is the father of all who believe and are justified.

Abraham: Our Father according to the Faith

THIS CHAPTER CONTINUES the discussion of Abraham in relation to justification. With Abraham's narrative from Genesis fresh in our minds, our attention now turns to Paul, with a particular focus on Romans 4. Here we examine:

- Justifying Ungodly Abraham
- The Imputation Question
- Therefore It Was Reckoned to Him: Romans 4:18–25
- Justification by Faith: Giving Glory to God
- Conclusion

No single figure, apart from Adam and Christ, is more central to biblical teaching on justification than Abraham. He is connected to virtually every aspect of the doctrine. For instance, Paul in Romans 4, on his way to discussing Adam, goes to Abraham to show that his ideas are not novel, that righteousness before God was always by faith and never by works. Abraham did not receive the promise on the basis of law but "through the righteousness of faith" (v. 13). In Galatians 3, Paul reminds his readers that they did not receive the Spirit by doing the works of the law but by faith, the same faith that God counted to Abraham as righteousness (vv. 5–6). Abraham is also called the father of all who believe, whether Jew or Gentile (Rom. 4:11–12; Gal. 3:7). It was through Abraham that

God began his faith-based nation building, making him "the father of many nations" (Rom. 4:17; cf. Gen. 17:5). The ancient gospel preached in Scripture—"In you shall all the nations of the earth be blessed" (Gal. 3:8; cf. Gen. 12:3)—prepared the way to "justify the Gentiles by faith" (Gal. 3:8). The story of Abraham shows that God's design all along was to display his grace through keeping his promise (Rom. 4:16; Gal. 3:18). If we understand Abraham the way Paul does, we will understand justifying faith in Christ.

Justifying Ungodly Abraham

Paul's view of Abraham fits both the Old Testament story and our story. Abraham is "the ungodly" one whom God justifies (Rom. 4:5). God chose an idol worshiper to become the father of many nations. We are like Abraham, being former idol worshipers who did not and could not find God on our own but must rely solely on his free grace. We are the nations who are blessed through Abraham, heirs according to the promise. Like Abraham, we have no personal claim to worthiness or righteousness; we only have faith in the promise-keeping God. The good news is that faith is all that is needed. Like Abraham, we are counted righteous by faith in the God who justifies the ungodly. The story of Abraham, and our story, is indeed about becoming the people of God, and it is also about being saved from our sins.[1]

No Works, No Exception

Paul begins Romans 4 by asking, "What then shall we say was gained by Abraham, our forefather according to the flesh?" (v. 1). Paul asks this question because he is about to show that what he has said up to this point about the justification of sinners

1. N. T. Wright often reminds us, as he does in his latest book, that Romans 4 is not *just* or *so much* about how Abraham or anyone else is saved or "gets justified" but about "God's faithfulness to his promises to Abraham." *Justification: God's Plan & Paul's Vision* (Downers Grove, IL: IVP, 2009), 222. I understand what he means, but we must keep and emphasize a "both/and" view.

by faith in Christ apart from the law (Rom. 3:21–31) is entirely biblical. In chapter 4, Paul continues to level the playing field for Jews and Gentiles. He started this in 1:16 by saying that the gospel is God's power of salvation for all believers, "to the Jew first and also to the Greek" (cf. 3:29–30). He has just said that all boasting is useless because justification is not by works but by faith (3:27), and he picks up that idea and proves it from Abraham. Paul's point is that God's righteousness revealed in the gospel was the same for Abraham. Paul underscores his point in chapter 4 when he reminds his readers that Abraham was justified *before* he was circumcised (v. 10). Circumcision was but a sign of the righteousness that he had by faith. In doing so, Paul knocks the legs out from under any idea that works or ethnic identity counts in God's judgment apart from faith. The point is that there is only one way to be justified, and it is through faith.

The Imputation Question

Anyone who works for a living can understand what Paul says in Romans 4:1–5. He takes his language from the marketplace, where wages are the just rewards for work. In verse 4, Paul states, "Now to the one who works, his wages are not counted as a gift but as his due." When a worker collects his check at the end of a pay period, he does not say to his boss, "Thank you for this thoughtful gift; my family can really use the money." While he may be grateful for the check, and though his family can use the money, he does not confuse it with a birthday present. The check is the agreed-upon payment for his work. There is a just exchange of labor for money. Paul contrasts the common practice of the marketplace with how Abraham was deemed righteous. When it comes to righteousness before God, it is all a gift.

Some Preliminary Matters

The doctrine of imputation is part but not the whole of justification. Imputation is the way righteousness is counted to us.

73

Justification is the verdict that through the work of God in Christ we stand before him without guilt and as having done all matters of obedience—we are declared righteous by God. That the righteousness counted to us is in fact God's righteousness in Christ is clear from 3:21–22: "But now the righteousness of God has been manifested apart from the law, although the Law and the Prophets bear witness to it—the righteousness of God through faith in Jesus Christ for all who believe."[2] The imputation of Christ's righteousness is the nuts and bolts of justification. That does not mean, however, that imputation is simply a matter of God's crunching numbers to make the justification equation add up—although some discussions make it sound that way. True, the picture in Romans 4:1–8 is of a ledger akin to a modern spreadsheet used in accounting or budgeting, but imputation is not a bloodless accounting of facts and figures. We must not lose sight of Christ, who lived and died for us and did everything necessary to move us from the debit to the credit side of the ledger.

What "Storehouse" of Merit? These days it is easy to get the impression that *everyone* who believes in imputation in any traditional sense must therefore believe that Jesus stored up a heavenly barn of righteousness to fork out to us as needed. There are many who hold to a traditional doctrine of imputation who *never* speak of it that way. Righteousness is not, after all, a commodity like grain stored in a silo. To use a different metaphor, there is no First National Bank of Heaven from which righteousness is withdrawn. The righteousness in view is incarnate, and imputation is sharing in the Christ who is our righteousness. Yes, people have spoken of it that way, just as some theologians speak of the atonement as something that can be mathematically quantified, but the traditional view of imputation is not grounded in a metaphor. Whatever the case, everyone should be able to recognize

2. I continue (with a shrinking majority of readers) to interpret the phrase as "faith *in* Christ" rather than "the faithfulness of Christ," although there are good arguments for the latter interpretation. Even if it were "the faithfulness of Christ," it is still God's righteousness displayed in Christ. Interested readers should see *The Faith of Jesus Christ*, ed. Michael F. Bird and Preston M. Sprinkle (Peabody, MA/Milton Keys, UK: Hendrickson/Paternoster, 2009).

that the storehouse language is an attempt, however inaccurate, to describe the sufficiency of the work of Christ on our behalf. It is simply a metaphor, much as the "fountain of righteousness" found in one of the Dead Sea Scrolls is a metaphor for divine wisdom.[3] I am quite sure that the writer of that scroll did not imagine he was speaking comprehensively of divine wisdom or had concluded that wisdom is simply an objective thing that God pours out like buckets filled from a fountain. To date, no one has overthrown the concept of wisdom in the Dead Sea Scrolls based on one metaphor.

Positive and Negative. Theologians have spoken of both a positive and a negative side to the imputation of Christ's righteousness.[4] There is a positive imputation of righteousness and a negative removal of sin (the nonimputation of sin). Like the way Christ's obedience is sometimes described, the positive has to do with his fulfillment of God's commands and the negative with his death on the cross. The former renders to believers a positive status before God as those who obeyed, and the latter grants forgiveness of sins. But as with Christ's obedience—and imputation is the reckoning of that obedience and what it attained to the believer—the positive and negative aspects of imputation cannot be separated. Christ's total work counts to make the believer righteous. The reckoning of righteousness and forgiveness are two sides of the same imputation coin.

Faith, Forgiveness, and Justification

The key word in this text is *counted* (*logizomai*), sometimes translated as *reckoned* and from which we get the concept of imputation.[5] Paul contrasts two kinds of counting. In the first instance, wages are counted as the reward for works; in the second,

3. IQS 11:6–8.
4. *Positive* and *negative* can be a little confusing since we typically associate those terms with good and bad unless we are speaking of batteries. In this discussion they are both good, with *negative* referring to something being taken away, namely sin.
5. The following section tracks loosely with the discussion in Brian Vickers, *Jesus' Blood and Righteousness: Paul's Theology of Imputation* (Wheaton, IL: Crossway, 2006), 91–111.

faith is counted as righteousness. This immediately raises an important question: Is faith in Christ a replacement for works? Just as works are rewarded with what is due, is faith rewarded with righteousness? This is not the way that Paul describes it. First, Paul is *contrasting* two things, not simply swapping one for the other. One thing is owed and counted for what it is, while the other is received by grace as a gift and counts for something else. Wages are counted for what is earned while faith is counted as righteousness, a gift that comes to the undeserving and ungodly.

Second, faith must not be thought of apart from its object. The righteousness in view is not made up of faith but is found in faith's object. Paul does not say that justification is *because* of faith but *by* faith.[6] Faith is the means by which we are made right with God through Christ, the object of faith and the foundation of our righteousness. Here are some examples of faith as a means or instrument in Romans.

> [Christ,] whom God put forward as a propitiation by his blood, to be received **by faith**. This was to show God's righteousness, because in his divine forbearance he had passed over former sins. It was to show his righteousness at the present time, so that he might be just and the justifier of *the one who has faith in Jesus*. (3:25–26)

> Therefore, since we have been justified **by faith**, we have peace with God through our Lord Jesus Christ. Through him we have also obtained access **by faith** into this grace in which we stand, and we rejoice in hope of the glory of God. (5:1–2)

> What shall we say, then? That Gentiles who did not pursue righteousness have attained it, that is, a righteousness that is **by faith**? (9:30)

Even when Paul speaks of "the righteousness *based on faith*" (10:6), he is not speaking of faith as an ultimate basis for righ-

---

6. John Murray, *Redemption Accomplished and Applied* (Grand Rapids: Eerdmans, 1955), 125.

teousness but is contrasting the law and faith as opposing ways of attaining righteousness.[7] The law is about attaining righteousness through doing commands (v. 5), but "the goal of the law is Christ for righteousness for everyone who believes" (v. 4, my translation).[8] Paul accuses the Jews of trying to establish their own righteousness based on *doing*, but the Gentiles attain God's righteousness based on believing in Christ for their righteousness. Paul contrasts faith and works and how each operates and attains its goal. Faith is not the new covenant version of works.

Faith is what unites us to God's righteousness, so when Paul says that Abraham's faith was *counted* as righteousness, he means specifically that his faith *in God* was counted as righteousness. If faith is the righteousness in question, then faith is really a work. But Paul presents the righteousness reckoned to Abraham not as his own but as something that comes by grace. It is the justification of the *ungodly* that is in view here; they are justified by believing in him who justifies the ungodly.

Faith is at best vague and at worst meaningless apart from its object. Talk show hosts may introduce a guest as "a person of faith," and politicians and other public figures may talk about how their "faith" keeps them "grounded" or keeps them "going," but unless faith is grounded in Christ, the focus is on the strength, attributes, or perseverance of the person who has "faith"—the very opposite of the way in which the Bible speaks of faith. Christians must avoid speaking of faith in this bland and generic way at all costs. Faith in Christ boasts in him, not in itself. People do not need to hear about our faith—they need to hear about the one in whom we place our faith.

Imputation according to David. In Romans 4:6–8, Paul brings in Old Testament support.

> David also speaks of the blessing of the one to whom God counts righteousness apart from works: "Blessed are those whose

---

7. Faith as a means of righteousness is established in context in 9:30.

8. My translation is identical to John Piper's translation in *Counted Righteous in Christ: Shall We Abandon the Imputation of Christ's Righteousness?* (Wheaton, IL: Crossway, 2002), 87.

lawless deeds are forgiven, and whose sins are covered; blessed is the man against whom the Lord will not count his sin."

Quoting the Old Testament like this is Paul's way of saying, "Here is what I mean." The word that stands out in the quote is *count* ("will not count his sin"). In Psalm 32, it refers to what is sometimes called the *nonimputation* of sin, which is basically a technical word for forgiveness meant to clarify the full justifying work of Christ. The two other descriptions also focus on forgiveness: "those whose lawless deeds are forgiven, and whose sins are covered." The quote refers explicitly to forgiveness more than it does to the counting of a positive status. The context of Psalm 32 follows suit as David speaks of wasting away because of his sin and of feeling the weight of God's hand of judgment until he confesses and receives forgiveness (vv. 3–5). Yet the psalm ends with a further description of those forgiven of their sins. David concludes with this confident declaration of those who believe God: "Many are the sorrows of the wicked, but steadfast love surrounds the one who trusts in the Lord. Be glad in the Lord, and rejoice, O righteous, and shout for joy, all you upright in heart!" (vv. 10–11). It is believers who enjoy the blessing of forgiveness, experience the love of God, and are called righteous and the upright. It is worthwhile to consider the larger context and language of Psalm 32 at this point.

Doing What Is Right in the Eyes of the Lord. When someone is said to be upright, it refers to behavior and/or what characterizes a person. For instance, God himself and his acts, law, and words are upright.[9] It describes those who obey God's commandments: "You shall diligently keep the commandments of the Lord your God. . . . And you shall do *what is right* and good in the sight of the Lord" (Deut. 6:17–18). It relates to kings who were characterized by obedience to God and his law and by opposition to idolatry,

---

9. Hannes Oliver, "yashar," in *New International Dictionary of Old Testament Theology and Exegesis*, vol. 2, ed. Willem A. VanGemeren (Grand Rapids: Zondervan, 1997), 566. Oliver cites the following texts: Deut. 32:4; Neh. 9:13; Pss. 19:9; 33:4; 92:15; 111:8; 119:137; Hos. 14:9.

who followed in the footsteps of David, "who kept my command-ments and followed me with all his heart, doing only that which was right in my eyes" (1 Kings 14:8).[10] The word is also paired with *righteous* in other texts.[11]

These two words are together in the famous passage in Habakkuk 2: "Behold, his soul is puffed up; it is not upright within him, but the righteous shall live by his faith" (v. 4). Here the one who is "not upright" is set over against "the righteous," contrast-ing the life of faith with the life of the wicked. It is difficult not to see something more than forgiveness in the description "righ-teous" and "upright." Psalm 32 begins with a blessing spoken on the forgiven person and ends with a word to people whose lives are marked by the actions of those who believe God and live in light of his loving kindness. Psalm 32, the source of Paul's quote, links the ideas of forgiveness and a positive standing before God closely together, providing even more support that the two are not separate but equal.

Erasing and Crediting: Heavenly Accounting. Paul says that David "speaks of the blessing of the one to whom God counts righ-teousness apart from works" (Rom. 4:6). The one counted with righteousness is the one whose sins are forgiven. He is the same person. The question is whether the counting of righteousness and the blessing of forgiveness are the same thing. In a word, no. In the immediate context Paul pits works against faith *as a way of being justified*: Abraham could boast if he was justified by works (v. 2); however, he did not work but believed, and so God credited him with righteousness (v. 3). A worker earns his wages (v. 4), but the one who does not work but believes is credited with righteousness (v. 5).

As we take in a little more context, we see that the contrast continues as Paul sets *the righteousness of faith* over against cir-cumcision (vv. 9–11) and law (vv. 13–15). Here circumcision and

10. Ibid., citing Deut. 12:28; 13:18; 1 Kings 11:38; 15:11; 22:43; 2 Kings 12:2; 2 Chron. 14:2; 20:32; 24:2.
11. As is the case in Ps. 32, these two words are together in other psalms when contrasting the righteous and upright with the wicked, such as 64:10; 94:15; 97:11. Also see Prov. 21:18.

the law are set out as contrary to faith for the *positive* counting of righteousness. Abraham already had the righteousness of faith before he was circumcised (v. 11). His obedience in circumcision did not count for righteousness but was a sign of it. The promise to Abraham and his children did not come through the law but through the righteousness of faith (v. 13). The blessing of justification cannot come through the law because law only brings wrath (v. 15); the implication is that righteousness through the law is impossible.[12] In context, *doing* and *believing* are presented as alternative ways of gaining God's declaration of righteousness—the status of one who has lived up to God's perfect standards. Only one of them, however, counts before God.

The upshot is that even though forgiveness receives emphasis, works are not contrasted with forgiveness alone. Any reckoning of righteousness must include a positive imputation of righteousness as part of being justified. Paul is speaking of *earning* the positive status of righteousness in contrast with faith counted as righteousness—also a positive status. Think again of an accounting ledger: there is not only a debit side so that you are either in the red or breaking even, but both a debit side and a credit side. Here, the debit is sin and the credit is righteousness. Debts must be paid for anything to show up on the credit side, but paying debt alone will not put a mark on the positive side. If a business earns $1000 in sales but has $2000 in overhead, the accountant will not report a gain—the company is still $1000 in the hole. If the same business reported $2000 in sales with $2000 in overhead, there would still be no entry in the credit column because the firm did not make a profit but simply broke even. Of course it is good to break even and certainly much better than having debt, but the company with $2000 in overhead needs to bring in at least $2001 for a number to show up on the positive side of the ledger. In terms of imputation, sin must be erased from the debit side of the ledger *and* an entry must be made on the positive side.

12. Thomas R. Schreiner, *Romans*, Baker Exegetical Commentary (Grand Rapids: Baker, 1998), 230.

Giving Emphasis Where Emphasis Is Due. Even though justi-fication consists of both forgiveness and the imputation of positive righteousness, it is still the case that one side or the other can receive emphasis. In Romans 4, forgiveness receives more explicit emphasis than positive imputation. One implies the other, but that does not mean they are always equally explicit, or that we have to make them that way in a particular text. While texts must be read together, we will not give individual texts their due unless we read them in their own right before explaining what is implied by larger biblical-theological considerations. Like the imputation of positive righteousness, forgiveness must be emphasized as it is in the Bible and never marginalized, even unintentionally. This idea is worth developing, so a cautionary detour from Paul's story of Abraham in Romans 4 is in order.

Speaking of Forgiveness. Some time ago I heard a man pray. Duly thanking God for salvation, he repeated the phrase *the impu-tation of Christ's righteousness* several times. It is entirely appro-priate to be thankful for Christ's imputed righteousness, but it struck me that there was no mention whatsoever of forgiveness, although virtually every other aspect of salvation made the prayer/lecture list. I often hear talk of imputation—some people even write books about it—yet comparatively little about forgiveness. Of course, when imputation is attacked and forgiveness is pit-ted against it, attention will turn to imputation. This is nothing new, for many people have questioned imputation and considered forgiveness as the whole of justification.[13] However, debates and sharp disagreements often lead to a pendulum swing. At one end of the arc is the denial of imputation, but when the pendulum swings to the extreme other side, forgiveness gets short shrift.

In the history of Protestant, particularly Reformed, theology, the word *mere* is often used to describe forgiveness in discus-sions about justification. Depending on one's context, however, *mere* may not communicate what is intended. These days the

13. Carl R. Trueman points out that there were even some among the Westminster Assembly (1643) who held only to the imputation of Christ's passive obedience; "Reformed Orthodoxy in Britain," *The Southern Baptist Journal of Theology* 14, 4 (2010): 11–12.

word *mere* typically has a more negative tone than it once did. If I say, "He owes me a mere dollar," I mean that the amount I am owed is insignificant. The comment might be accompanied by a dismissive wave of the hand. If I used the word *measly*, it would mean the same thing to most people. We almost always use *only* rather than *mere*. When theologians say "mere forgiveness is not enough for justification," they mean "forgiveness *by itself* is not the whole of justification." That is right, but it does not come across that way now in every setting. We have to be careful that we neither practically de-emphasize forgiveness in efforts to uphold another vital biblical doctrine nor mistakenly speak of it in ways that downplay the astonishing truth that in Christ our sins are forgiven.

The Broad Horizon of Forgiveness. There must be a good reason why John Calvin, commenting on the quote from Psalm 32 in Romans 4, could say, "By these words we also learn that righteousness for Paul is nothing other than the remission of sins. . . . We are therefore left with the glorious statement that he who is cleansed before God by the free remission of sins is justified by faith."[14] Likewise, John Murray speaks of Paul's "more restricted interest" in forgiveness in Romans 4 and notes that in this text justification is parallel to, "if not defined in terms of, the remission of sins."[15] Let us be clear: neither Calvin nor Murray equates forgiveness and justification, but it is equally important to understand that they both recognize the special emphasis that forgiveness receives in Romans 4 via the quote from Psalm 32. Just as the imputation of righteousness from a traditional view assumes forgiveness, so forgiveness may assume imputation.

Centrality of Forgiveness. Forgiveness is tied to every aspect of life with God in the Old Testament. First, God is presented as the God who forgives. When God reveals himself to Moses in Exodus 34, he declares that he forgives "iniquity and transgression

14. John Calvin, *Romans and Thessalonians*, Calvin's New Testament Commentaries, trans. Ross Mackenzie, ed. David W. Torrance and Thomas F. Torrance (Grand Rapids/Carlisle, UK: Baker/Paternoster, 1995), 86.

15. John Murray, *Romans*, New International Commentary on the New Testament, ed. F. F. Bruce (Grand Rapids: Eerdmans, 1959), 134.

and sin" (v. 7). In Numbers 14, when the people are clamoring to go back to Egypt after hearing the report about giants in the Promised Land, Moses pleads with God not to punish them but to "pardon the iniquity of this people, according to the greatness of your steadfast love" (v. 19).

Second, there is a definite emphasis on forgiveness as what is needed to mend a broken relationship with God. What comes to mind first is the number of sacrificial texts that focus exclusively on forgiveness. When a bull is sacrificed as a sin offering for the nation and the priest makes atonement, "they shall be forgiven" (Lev. 4:20). Likewise, when an individual sins, a burnt offering may be made for him, and "he shall be forgiven" (v. 35).[16] When the people are consumed with sin, they are unable to serve God, as Joshua makes clear to the early Canaan settlers: "You are not able to serve the LORD, for he is a holy God. He is a jealous God; he will not forgive your transgressions or your sins" (Josh. 24:19). When David's sin is exposed, he knows that his only hope is forgiveness: "Wash me thoroughly from my iniquity, and cleanse me from my sin! For I know my transgressions, and my sin is ever before me" (Ps. 51:2–3).

Third, the future hope of God's people rests on forgiveness, as God promises that a time will come when he will write his law on their hearts and everyone will have a personal knowledge of him; it will happen because he will forgive their sins once and for all: "For I will forgive their iniquity, and I will remember their sin no more" (Jer. 31:34). Texts could be multiplied exponentially, but the point is that often the Old Testament emphasizes forgiveness as what puts people in a right relationship with God.

The conclusion to draw, however, is not that forgiveness was central in the Mosaic covenant and then positive imputation came along later. For one, Abraham predates the law, and righteousness before God was always credited through faith. Second, the need to be righteous before God was ever present, as the law made clear. The forgiveness underscored continually in the Old Testament is

16. Other examples can be found in Lev. 4:26, 31; 5:10, 13, 16, 18; 6:7; 19:22.

required because of disobedience. When God revealed himself as a God of forgiveness, when he forgave through the sacrifices, and when he promised to forgive in the future, it was all against the backdrop of disobedience, a failure to do God's will that reached all the way back to Adam's disobedience. So while forgiveness is emphasized and may be the primary thing mentioned in a text, justification before God always assumes positive obedience, not only the erasing of the debit side of the ledger.

Justifying Blood. The New Testament also contains texts that speak broadly of forgiveness even in connection to righteousness and justification. The one that stands out is Romans 5:9: "Since, therefore, we have now been justified by his blood, much more shall we be saved by him from the wrath of God." There is no doubt that "blood" in this verse refers to forgiveness through the atoning sacrifice of Christ on the cross (cf. 3:25). To say we are "justified by his blood" does not have to equate forgiveness with justification, but it does emphasize that there must be forgiveness of sins for anyone to be justified. It makes sense for Paul to speak of forgiveness in such sweeping terms since the context is all about Christ's dying to save sinners and so reconcile God with those who have sinned against him. Paul, in fact, closely ties justification (5:1) with reconciliation (v. 10) to underscore what Christ accomplished in his death for sinners (v. 8).

As with 3:21–26, this text rests on the Old Testament sacrificial background, where forgiveness is the key to a restored relationship between God and man. Here the key is "the death of his Son" and also the resurrected life of the Son through which God's people will be saved from the coming judgment (5:10). It is no accident that Paul will shortly turn his attention to Christ the true Adam, who through obedience brings eternal life over against the judgment of death that followed Adam. Before he gets to Adam, Paul presents Christ as the one who gained eternal life for those who believe in him. The sin that brought God's wrath has been forgiven through the new Adam, and what is more, the life promised in Eden has become a reality not just through the death of Christ but through his life as well.

Justifying Mercy. Another well-known text that links justification and forgiveness is the parable of the Pharisee and the tax collector. In the story the Pharisee is a prime example of what Paul talks about in Romans 10:1–5. He establishes his own righteousness based on what he does not do (extort money, act unjustly, commit adultery, or live like the tax collector) and what he does do (fasting and tithing). Although he does acknowledge or at least give the required nod to God by beginning his prayer with, "God, I thank you," he counts on his own righteousness and even stands off by himself a bit where he is likely to get attention. The tax collector, however, humbles himself, beats his chest, and cries, "God, be merciful to me, a sinner!" What was Jesus' verdict? "I tell you, this man went down to his house justified, rather than the other" (Luke 18:14). The implication is that the tax collector was forgiven upon his repentance and his trust in God's mercy. Jesus simply says that he was justified. There is no mention of any sort of positive reckoning on the ledger. But why should there be? First off, it is not a treatise on soteriology but a story that makes a comparison in order to teach something vital. Luke tells us that Jesus told this parable specifically to people "who trusted in themselves that they were righteous, and treated others with contempt" (v. 9). It was meant for people who were just like the Pharisee in the parable; it is not a detached theological tidbit.

The parable contrasts righteousness before God on the basis of works and on the basis of repentant faith. One man looks inward while the other looks outward. The Pharisee looks at himself and says, "God, look how good I am!," while the tax collector, despairing over his sin so much that he is ashamed to look up to heaven, says, "God, help me!" It is a tale of two kinds of righteousness: one by works and the other by faith, although the former is not righteousness at all. Ultimately it is about the sin of self-righteousness in contrast with righteousness through faith. That every aspect of justification is not spelled out is hardly surprising given the context. The parable is exactly in keeping with the biblical doctrine of justification by faith alone, but the fullness of the doctrine comes from the entire Bible, not one parable.

Justifying Sacrifice. Second Corinthians 5:21 is one of the texts at the heart of the biblical teaching on justification: "For our sake he made him to be sin who knew no sin, so that in him we might become the righteousness of God." In union with Christ, believers share in God's righteousness. That righteousness was displayed in the judgment and salvation of the cross. Because of what Christ has done, God identifies those in Christ as having his righteousness, that is, as having Christ himself. In the eyes of God, what is true of Christ is true of those who believe in him, and this takes place as a result of Christ's substitutionary death on the cross. Drawing broadly on the Old Testament, Paul presents Christ as the perfect sacrifice without blemish[17] ("knew no sin") by which God and man are reconciled. It is the forgiveness that flows from the sacrifice of Christ whom God "made . . . to be sin" that causes believers to "become the righteousness of God."

Paul not only highlights forgiveness in verse 21, but he also speaks in verse 19 of God's "not counting their trespasses," a phrase similar to the accounting language found in Romans 4:2–6 with emphasis on erasure of the debit side of the ledger. The focus of this text is not surprising given that Paul is pleading for his readers to be reconciled to God, a relationship that results from forgiveness. Still, there are hints of a larger view in the context. Becoming the righteousness of God in Christ is linked directly to being "a new creation," and so as in Romans 5:10, 18, and 21, the idea of a life connected to obedience from Adam onward is present in a text focused on justification—but there is no getting around the fact that forgiveness is the key issue. This text is a prime example of how biblical doctrine does not hinge on a single verse but is built upon the foundation of texts, and each text should be allowed to speak in its own right.

Even though only a small number of texts from the Old Testament and the New Testament were considered, I hope there is enough evidence to keep us from unintentionally downgrading

---

17. Lev. 4:3; 5:15, 18; 6:6; 9:2–3. These are among texts cited in the full discussion of the Old Testament background for "made . . . to be sin" in Vickers, *Jesus' Blood and Righteousness*, 160–70.

forgiveness when teaching and preaching on justification. Now we will get back to Paul's story of Abraham.

Therefore It Was Reckoned to Him: Romans 4:18–25

All too often readers with particular interest in justification pull up from Romans 4 when the Psalm 32 quote ends in verse 8. But Paul is not done with Abraham. He gives a brief theological summary of Abraham's life, then does something that might strike readers as at least surprising—he quotes Genesis 15:6 again. This time he does so *after* fast-forwarding Abraham's life beyond the night outside his tent. Paul presents Abraham as both the model of the just one who lives by faith and as the one through whom God's redemption unfolds. Abraham's faith took real form in his life, and in doing so proved not only that he was justified but also that God is trustworthy and true to his word.

The Just One Lives by Faith

In two places Paul quotes Habakkuk 2:4, "the righteous shall live by faith." In both places, Romans 1:17 and Galatians 3:11, Abraham is in the vicinity. In Galatians, Abraham is in the immediate context, while in Romans the distance between the quote and the appearance of Abraham is fairly large. The content of the larger context of Romans, however, brings the two closer than they may appear at first.

Romans 1:16–17 is arguably the main idea in Romans, and after showing the sinfulness of both Gentiles and Jews, Paul comes full circle to show that the revelation of God's righteousness in Christ is the answer for both Jew and Gentile (3:21–31): justification is a gift of God's grace to all who believe in Christ Jesus. Paul's discussion of Abraham flows directly from the last verses of chapter 3. So Abraham is not all that remote from the Habakkuk quote in Romans. The content shared with Galatians 3 also supports connecting Abraham to the Habakkuk quote in Romans. Consider just some of the parallels.

Abraham "the Just" in Romans and Galatians

Quote of Genesis 15:6	Romans 4:3	Galatians 3:6
Promise of Nation/Seed	Romans 4:18	Galatians 3:8
Children by Faith	Romans 4:12, 16	Galatians 3:7, 9
Curse/Wrath of Law	Romans 4:15	Galatians 3:10

More parallels can be drawn but, in short, Paul contrasts justification by faith with works/works of the law; Abraham is in the thick of the argument in both letters, with the quote from Habakkuk 2:4 as a kind of lens to use in reading him.[18] In Romans 4, Paul goes on to speak of what that looks like in the life of Abraham and how it connects to the reckoning of righteousness.

Hoping against Hope

Paul speaks of the justification of Abraham in the context of creation out of nothing. Abraham believed in the God "who gives life to the dead and calls into existence the things that do not exist" (4:17). God called an ungodly idol worshiper and made him the father of many nations, and in a dead womb God created the seed through which the entire world would be blessed—all this in the face of overwhelming evidence to the contrary. When Paul says that Abraham "in hope believed against hope," he means that Abraham persevered in faith even though the situation was hopeless. Because of the speed of the story in Genesis, it is easy to forget that over twenty-five years

18. There is an enormous amount of literature dealing with Paul's interpretation and use of Habakkuk. This is not the place to pursue the exegetical debates (important though they are), but for an excellent and accessible survey of the issues involved see Thomas R. Schreiner, *Galatians*, Exegetical Commentary on the New Testament (Grand Rapids: Zondervan, 2010), 207–10. Mark A. Seifrid has a particularly engaging discussion of this text in "Romans," in *Commentary on the New Testament Use of the Old Testament*, ed. Gregory K. Beale and D. A. Carson (Grand Rapids: Baker, 2007), 608–11.

passed between God's giving the promise and his fulfilling it. Twenty-five years by itself is a long time, but with a barren wife and he being past his sell-by date, being a hundred years old by the time Isaac was conceived, it must have seemed like forever.

Many of us find it hard to believe God and his promises even for a matter of months or days unless we see some concrete evidence. Whether it is an answer to prayer (typically counted as such when our desires are met), a confirmation that we made the right decision about a job, or a turn in our health or finances, we look for something tangible, putting confidence in things seen rather than things unseen.[19] For most of us it takes something less than twenty-five years to entertain some doubts. It would hardly take twenty-five years for someone to say, "I don't think God is in this." Given Abraham's actions, at times it seems that he experienced something akin to this too. Paul, however, takes the long view of Abraham's life and says:

> He did not weaken in faith when he considered his own body, which was as good as dead (since he was about a hundred years old), or when he considered the barrenness of Sarah's womb. No distrust made him waver concerning the promise of God, but he grew strong in his faith as he gave glory to God. (4:19–20)

How can Paul say such things? With Abraham's tendency to put his wife's virtue on the line to save his own skin (Gen. 12:11–13; chapter 20), the doubt he expresses in God's promise when he reminds God that he still does not have a child and that Eliezer will be his heir (15:2), and his decision to go along with Sarah's plan to make an heir through Hagar (chapter 16), it may seem that Paul is sugarcoating things a bit. Such a conclusion, although understandable on the surface, is off base. Paul certainly knew the details of Abraham's life, but he was not looking for perfect faith, the kind that never entertains a shred of doubt or fear, but persevering faith in the justifying God that keeps on in the face of doubt and fear. Perseverance over time,

---

19. I.e., the opposite of the way Heb. 11:1 describes faith.

not perfection, is the fruit of faith—perfection must wait until faith and hope are realized.

Therefore Genesis 15:6 Is True

In Romans 4:22, Paul draws the conclusion from his summary of Abraham's life of faith (vv. 18–21).[20] When Paul quotes Genesis 15:6 for a second time (Rom. 4:22), it confirms two things: (1) Abraham's life of faith was the evidence of his justification; and (2) what God in Scripture declared about Abraham was true. The ESV captures the idea: "That is why his faith was 'counted to him as righteousness.'"[21] A paraphrase of the verse might go something like this: "You can see from Abraham's perseverance that truly his faith was reckoned as righteousness in Genesis 15:6." It is not that Abraham's justification was provisional or partial but that Abraham's life (marked by believing God, not wavering, growing strong in faith, and giving glory to God) is like evidence in a courtroom that supports a plea. This is not, however, identical to any human courtroom.

Believing in Justification by Faith. When a plaintiff enters a plea of "not guilty" and then the evidence shows he was nowhere near the crime scene, his fingerprints were not found, and he has a solid alibi, the jury comes back from deliberation and says "not guilty" (the plea is true). In our law courts, the evidence must necessarily come before the verdict. However, in the case of Abraham, the verdict did not await evidence to support a plea but was declared before the evidence was given. Abraham's faith was counted as righteousness *before*, and not on the basis of, the evidence shown in his life. The initial verdict passed on Abraham and on all believers is not a public verdict (that verdict will come in the future) but one known by faith alone: "for with the heart one believes and is justified" (Rom. 10:10), yet it is a real verdict nonetheless. It

---

20. Douglas J. Moo, *Romans*, New International Commentary on the New Testament (Grand Rapids: Eerdmans, 1996), 286.

21. The NIV is almost identical, translating the Greek *dio* (*wherefore*; *therefore*) as "this is why."

is real because it is based on the finished work of Christ, and because of that work we can have assurance of the verdict now. Of course God, who knows the end from the beginning, also knows the confirming evidence that will flow from faith, but the declaration of justification is founded in Christ alone, the object of faith.

Believing that one is justified in the sight of God is part of living by faith. The believer *believes* that he is justified by God in the present—it is not just hope in a purely future verdict that may or may not be realized depending on one's works. If that were the case, then we would receive everything that has to do with God's salvation in Christ by faith except for justification itself. Paul, however, says in Romans 5:1–2 that we are justified and have peace with God in the present, and because of that we have certain hope for the future. The hope of justification is that we will stand before God and hear publicly the final verdict of righteousness which is spoken to us now through faith. Justification by faith situates the believer simultaneously in the present, past, and future. Faith looks to God's promises, the guarantee and fulfillment of which is the cross, and lays hold of them in the present.

The meeting of the past, present, and future in justification is borne out in the following verses. Paul immediately applies the justification of Abraham to the justification of all believers in 4:23–25. The story of Abraham in Genesis was written for all who would believe in Jesus.

> But the words "it was counted to him" were not written for his sake alone, but for ours also. It will be counted to us who believe in him who raised from the dead Jesus our Lord, who was delivered up for our trespasses and raised for our justification.

What Abraham had in a promise we have in its fulfillment. Abraham believed in the One "who gives life to the dead" (v. 17), and now we believe in that same God who raised Jesus from the dead in fulfillment of his promise—the future promised to Abraham began with

91

the resurrection of Jesus.[22] Jesus stood in God's court, received the guilty sentence that was ours, and died for our sins. Then God the Judge declared the penalty paid and raised Jesus from the grave so that we could receive the verdict of righteousness and hope for the future, just as Abraham hoped in God's future and persevered by faith because of it.

Justification by Faith: Giving Glory to God

What stands out in the text is not the perfection of Abraham's faith but the perfection of the One in whom Abraham believed. In the final analysis this passage is about the God who forgives and reckons righteousness, and his faithfulness to his word and worthiness to be trusted. If we read Romans 4 and miss the grand picture of God in the text and focus solely on Abraham, ourselves, or general ideas about justification, then we miss the text entirely. Abraham's justifying faith is anchored in God.

The Glory of God in Romans 4

- The God who justifies the ungodly
- The God who gives life to the dead
- The God who creates from nothing
- The God who can be trusted
- The God who gets all the glory

The story of Abraham, like the doctrine of justification itself, is a story that points all attention to God. An old man, a barren woman, imperfect human beings, overwhelming odds, and years of waiting build the stage on which God, in both his word and his actions, receives all the glory. Subsequently his people receive all the benefits, chiefly the gift of being

22. Schreiner, *Romans*, 242.

declared righteous and the confidence of knowing that what God says is true.

Conclusion

Through Abraham we learn that God does not justify anyone on the basis of works but through faith alone. Through Abraham we learn that it is faith, not works, that God counts as righteousness. Faith, however, is not a new "work" but is what unites us to Christ, the source of our righteousness. The righteousness provided by Christ the last Adam is applied to us through faith. In this way we could think of Paul's teaching on Abraham as functioning as the application of his Adam/Christ theology. Christ, through his obedience, provides the righteousness that we, the children of Adam, need in order to stand before God. He is also the fulfillment of God's promise, and through faith we share his obedience-won righteousness.

5

The Law: Things by Which You Cannot Be Justified

"Run, John, run," the law commands but gives us neither feet nor hands. —John Bunyan[1]

THERE IS NO WAY AROUND IT: understanding the law, its place in the Scripture, and its role in redemption is difficult. But when we miss the point that the law is neither an end nor a beginning but a crucial step in God's redemption, we contribute to the difficulty. The law teaches us a great deal about who God is, what he requires, and what it takes to be righteous in his sight. It also teaches us about ourselves as it reveals sin and the inability of human beings under Adam's curse to be righteous through law-keeping. Because of all this, knowledge of the law in its Old Testament context is necessary for understanding New Testament texts that speak of God's righteousness and our justification. The goal of this chapter is to deal, however briefly, with the law in its narrative, covenantal, and redemptive-historical contexts. The aim is to see how the Bible describes the law and to identify its main

---

1. Although he is often credited for this quote, there is uncertainty whether it really came from John Bunyan.

purposes in light of the larger discussion of justification. We will focus on:

- Ground Rules
- Holy, Just, and Good: An Overview of the Law
- Obedience through Dependence: Psalm 119:32–37
- The Covenant and Redemption
- Conclusion

Ground Rules

When I see an acorn, I do not pretend that I have never seen an oak tree. When I read the Old Testament, I do not act as though I have not read the New Testament. This is not the place, nor is there space, to pursue a full contextual study of the Mosaic law in general, so before going further I want to spell out a basic idea that guides this chapter. The Old Testament, including the law, *is fully understood only in light of the New Testament*. Reading every biblical text in its own context is necessary for sound interpretation, but there are many layers of context, and the ultimate context is the whole Bible. The New Testament writers present themselves and the church of Christ as the inheritors of the Old Testament story, as those living in the era of fulfillment. The Old Testament itself looks forward to this fulfillment and promises its coming. In short, this chapter, like the chapters on Adam and Abraham, takes an end-from-the-beginning perspective.

The Big Picture: Israel-in-Adam

Discussions about keeping the law or righteousness through law-keeping must ultimately take into account the larger story of the Bible forward and backward. The law was given to people living under the curse of Genesis 3. The law hits Israel-in-Adam like a Hummer hitting a Smart Car—there is little doubt about the outcome. By "in Adam" I mean that Israel is born outside the garden, apart from the direct presence of God and under the curse of Adam's guilt and sin. True, they are children of Abraham and in line to receive God's promise and are themselves a fulfillment of the promise, being already a great nation by the time they leave Egypt. They are also the means by which God carries forward his promise to its fulfillment in one "born under the law" (Gal. 4:4). Nevertheless, the fulfillment of the promise for a nation and to the nations is with those doing justice and righteousness (Gen. 18:19).[2] The law teaches justice and righteousness, but in Adam Israel is unable to attain the goal of the law.

Corporate and Individual

There is often disagreement over whether the Sinai covenant is corporately (communally) or individually focused. The answer is both. Although addressed primarily to a nation and a covenant community whose collective actions affect everyone, we cannot overlook the individual level. Each Israelite is responsible and accountable to God. Ezekiel makes this clear as he condemns the future use of this proverb as a crutch: "The fathers have eaten sour grapes, and the children's teeth are set on edge" (i.e., the father did something wrong and the children pay for it). To the contrary: "Behold, all souls are mine; the soul of the father as well as the soul of the son is mine: the soul who sins shall die" (Ezek. 18:4). Every individual, Israelites included, must stand before God (cf. 2 Cor. 5:10).

Yet the nature of Israel, being a covenant community, places emphasis on corporate obedience and disobedience.[3] Disobedience in the community, which does not mean the disobedience of everyone, is punished corporately. The best example of this is when both the northern and southern kingdoms were carried off into exile. All, even prophets like Jeremiah, suffer the consequences

2. Citing Gen. 18:18–19 and Jer. 4:1–2, Bauckham notes: "it is Israel's fulfillment of her covenant obligations, her practice of truth, justice, and righteousness that will bring blessing to the nations." Richard Bauckham, *Bible and Mission: Christian Mission in a Postmodern World* (Carlisle: Paternoster/Grand Rapids: Baker, 2003), 31.

3. Herman Bavinck, *Reformed Dogmatics*, vol. 3, *Sin and Salvation in Christ*, ed. John Bolt, trans. John Vriend (Grand Rapids: Baker, 2006), 34.

of the nation's sin. The Israelite community illustrates the corporate nature of covenant relationships. Individual actions affect everyone, including those who do not commit the acts themselves.

Tested for Obedience

In addition to Adam (Luke 3:38) and Christ (e.g., Matt. 14:33), Israel also is identified as God's son (Ex. 4:22). As with Adam and with Christ, there is a clear emphasis on obedience for Israel. As with the other two sons of God, testing for obedience has a prominent place in the life of Israel. As we saw earlier (chapter 1), it begins in Eden and continues on to Christ. Likewise, God tests Israel (e.g., Ex. 16:4) to see whether the nation will obey. In a sense the entire law can be viewed as a test for obedience. Taken as a whole and over the course of national history, and excepting a faithful remnant—people like Joshua, David, the prophets, and all those not mentioned by name—Israel's entire experience of the law demonstrates an inability to pass God's test of righteousness. Israel's failure to keep the law exposes the plight of the entire world before God.

Perfect Obedience

The law demands perfect obedience. Moses tells the people on many occasions to be "careful to obey *all* these words that I command you" (Deut. 12:28).[4] Perfect obedience was required in Eden and at Sinai.[5] Sometimes the words *perfect* and *imperfect* can be confusing because God did provide forgiveness through the sacrifices. We might conclude that God did not command perfect obedience, and made a way through the sacrificial system to make up for what was lacking in obedience. That conclusion, however, does not distinguish between what God commands and what he knows, and more importantly, what he planned. God commanded perfect obedience but knew that the people could not

---

4. See also Ex. 23:22; Deut. 11:13; 13:18; 15:5; 28:1, 15; 30:2, 8.
5. Thomas R. Schreiner, *40 Questions about Christians and Biblical Law* (Grand Rapids: Kregel, 2010), 53.

obey perfectly in and of themselves. He tells them as much from the beginning (Deut. 4:25–27). Did God, in this sense, command something that he knew the people could not do? Yes, he did. He did it to show what it means to be righteous in his eyes and what it takes to attain that righteousness. The sacrifices, which always pointed to something greater and were in themselves incapable of forgiving sin (Heb. 10:4), maintain the covenant relationship until the kind of obedience God requires is accomplished once for all. Ultimately it comes down to this: God commands that his people be holy as he is holy. Holiness, as we will see in a moment, is absolutely tied to perfection, the perfection of a life wholly devoted to God.

Holy, Just, and Good: An Overview of the Law

Commands, rules, and regulations are not bad things. One reason we have a negative view of the law is that our fallen minds associate commands for obedience with infringements on our personal rights and independence. Commands cramp our style—like the way I cramp my seven-year-old daughter's style when I tell her not to ride her bike into the street. We inherit our problem with commands and authority from our first father, and in turn have taken rebellion against all manner of laws and regulations, both natural and divine, to a new level (Rom. 1:18–32).

Beyond that, our negative views of the law are due to blaming the law for failing to perform what it was never meant to do. Yes, it commands obedience and lacks the power to bring about that obedience, but it was never meant to be the source of obedience. Paul does not condemn anyone for having a high regard for the law; he condemns people for trying to use the law to establish their own righteousness. The law does have a major negative role and purpose, but that does not make the law itself negative. It exposes our sin and points us to the Lawgiver. But even when it fulfills its condemning role of shining a spotlight on sin (Rom. 5:20; Gal. 3:19), it is doing something good for us:

it is causing us to look away from ourselves and to cry out for help (Rom. 7:24–25). If we view the law only in negative terms, we take a position that cannot be supported by the Bible. We can never forget that it is *God's* law, and even when the Bible speaks of "the" or "this" law, it is always the law of God. The law is holy, just, and good because its Giver is holy, just, and good.

The Law without the Lawgiver: Legalism

The main thing, however, that goes wrong in our thinking about the law is what went wrong for many Israelites, whether those wandering in the wilderness, going off as captives to Babylon, or, like the famous Pharisee from Tarsus who persecuted the Messiah: separate the law from God the Lawgiver. This is the essence of all ancient and modern legalism. Ignoring its covenantal-redemptive purpose, we think of the law as a thing in itself, a code to obey that will lead to a better life instead of the expressed word of the living God.[6] Once the law is separated from its biblical context, there is only one way to go—toward self-obsessed pride in our own accomplishments, particularly over against the moral failures of others. The remedy for all misunderstanding and confusion about the law begins with considering how the Bible speaks about it.

The Holiness and Wholeness of the Law

The law distinguished Israel, setting it apart from every nation on earth by defining its identity and bringing attention to the greatness of its God. Through Moses the Lord asks, "And what great nation is there, that has statutes and rules so righteous as all this law that I set before you today?" (Deut. 4:8). The giving of the law is an act of grace to Israel because it is set in the context of redemption from Egypt, functions as a response on

6. As Spykman notes, "The law of God loses its meaning apart from the biblical story line. For when we lift it out of its context in the history of redemption, we play into the hands of the Pharisees. . . . They converted the law into an independent and autonomous rule of conduct." Gordon J. Spykman, *Reformational Theology: A New Paradigm for Doing Dogmatics* (Grand Rapids: Eerdmans, 1992), 338.

Israel's part to its covenant relationship with God, reveals God's will, and displays his justice and care for his people even down to small details in their lives.[7] Through the law Israel learned that holiness before God is a *whole* life devoted to him. For instance, when God tells the Israelites how to tend their fruit trees, he is (1) teaching agronomy to a nation of ex-brickmakers with no farming experience; (2) showing them that every area of their lives is to be lived out in devotion to him; and (3) teaching that they are to live by faith—it is hard for a subsistence farmer to wait four years to pick fruit (see Lev. 19:23–25). The law also separated them from the surrounding pagan nations, not only in terms of social and sexual morality but also, for instance, in terms of appearance and practices.[8] Ultimately the law regulated the ways that Israel was to worship, serve, and live for the Lord. It was not simply a matter of keeping this or that law but a total way of life. It is not a list of things to do or avoid so much as a vision of what it means to live as the people of God. Far from being a practical guide for living, and apart from Israel's ability to keep it, the law informed, defined, regulated, maintained, and sustained the life of the people of God. It was his law for his people. The unity in the law, which directs attention to the intended unity of life, speaks to James's insistence that to break one commandment is to break all the commandments (James 2:10), and to Paul's point that taking on one command brings responsibility to keep all commands (Gal 5:3).

Dependence on God and Hope for the Future

"The law of the LORD is perfect, reviving the soul; the testimony of the LORD is sure, making wise the simple" (Ps. 19:7).

---

7. Dumbrell emphasizes recognition of the grace behind the giving of the law in its redemptive context as the proper covenant response on the part of Israel. William J. Dumbrell, *The Faith of Israel: Its Expression in the Books of the Old Testament* (Grand Rapids: Baker, 1988), 58.

8. Leviticus 19:28, for instance, forbids tattoos likely because tattooing was practiced by the nations with idolatrous connections and implications. It is similar to how in those days "graven images" were connected with pagan idolatry. Dismissing modern religious art out of hand misses the point of the command.

JUSTIFICATION BY GRACE THROUGH FAITH

The words of Psalm 19 show the esteem with which at least some Israelites held the law. The positive view of the law is best reflected in the Psalms, particularly the great ode to the law, Psalm 119. The law was the way of blessing, peace, and wisdom.

> Oh how I love your law! It is my meditation all the day. Your commandment makes me wiser than my enemies, for it is ever with me. I have more understanding than all my teachers, for your testimonies are my meditation. I understand more than the aged, for I keep your precepts. I hold back my feet from every evil way, in order to keep your word. I do not turn aside from your rules, for you have taught me. How sweet are your words to my taste, sweeter than honey to my mouth! Through your precepts I get understanding; therefore I hate every false way. Your word is a lamp to my feet and a light to my path. (Ps. 119:97–105)

This attitude about the law is the polar opposite of moralistic applications that seek to construct a "how-to" manual for living a good life. In Psalm 119, David does not speak of abstract principles by which life may be improved through moral principles and honest work, but of living in relationship with God. So often we speak of the law no differently than a book of virtues or a code of best practices—a "do this and you will live *well*" view—but this is not the way the Bible speaks of it. David never loses sight that it is "the law of the LORD," "his testimonies," and "his ways" (vv. 1–3), and that keeping the law is an act of, and leads to, worship: "I will praise you with an upright heart, when I learn your righteous rules" (v. 7). It does this because the law reveals both God and his intention for his people. It is the way for walking in obedience to God (v. 9) and dependence on God. The law does not cause David to put his shoulder to the wheel and nose to the grindstone but to turn to God as his only hope. For all his uprightness, there is never a hint of self-righteousness or self-reliance. He declares his righteousness in the face of enemy opposition, but he does not declare his righteousness in the face of God.[9] David prays to God: *"Open* my eyes, that I may behold wondrous things out of your law" (v. 18), and soon goes on to show that keeping the law is done only through the work of God.

Obedience through Dependence: Psalm 119:32–37

- I will run in the way of your commandments **when you enlarge my heart**!
- **Give me understanding**, that I may keep your law and observe it with my whole heart.
- **Lead me** in the path of your commandments, for I delight in it.
- **Incline my heart** to your testimonies, and not to selfish gain!
- **Turn my eyes** from looking at worthless things; and **give me life** in your ways.

Life in the community under the covenant law required dependence on the covenant God. The downgrade from law-keeping to legalism was never the intention.

The Promise in the Law. In addition to the theme of dependence, this hymn to God's law is attached to God's promise—a promise to act decisively in the future. There is little doubt that David spoke of temporal relief from his troubles and enemies, but there is a longing that stretches beyond the immediate time. David acknowledges that God is the Creator and that his word stands forever (vv. 89–90), and he looks forward to God's fulfilling of his word of promise: "My soul longs for your salvation; I hope in your word. My eyes long for your promise; I ask, 'When will you comfort me?'" (vv. 81–82). Later he sets his obedience in the context of hope in God's future: "I hope for your salvation, O

9. Geerhardus Vos, *The Eschatology of the Old Testament*, ed. James T. Dennison (Phillipsburg, NJ: P&R Publishing, 2001), 143.

JUSTIFICATION BY GRACE THROUGH FAITH

Lord, and I do your commandments" (v. 166), and finally, "I long for your salvation, O Lord, and your law is my delight" (v. 174). A clearer picture of what David longs for is seen when we read Psalm 119 the way all the psalms are meant to be read—in their larger context.[10]

Psalm 119 appears in the fifth book of the Psalter, which begins with Psalm 107 and a message of God's rescue of his people from exile. Psalm 108 praises God for his faithfulness to Israel and victory over her enemies. Prayers for mercy and for God's vengeance on her enemies fill Psalm 109. Then, dramatically, Psalm 110 promises a Priest-King who will sit on David's throne and judge the nations. The praise psalms that follow maintain the royal theme begun in Psalm 110. The intertwining of the themes of king and law is not new to the Old Testament. Deuteronomy 17 speaks of a future king who will rule according to the law and keep it perfectly. Psalms 1 and 2, read together, also connect the man who lives according to the law (Ps. 1) with the future king who will sit at God's right hand, judge his enemies, and rescue his people (Ps. 2). The point of all this is that the praise of the law found in Psalm 119 is tied to God's promise to act for the salvation of his people—law-keeping is set in the context of waiting for the fulfillment of God's word of promise to send a king who will keep the law and reign forever.

The New in the Old. The heart of the law is simple, at least in principle: love God and love your neighbor. When asked about the greatest commandment, Jesus answered:

> You shall love the Lord your God with all your heart and with all your soul and with all your mind. This is the great and first commandment. And a second is like it: You shall love your neighbor as yourself. On these two commandments depend all the Law and the Prophets. (Matt. 22:37–40)

10. This contextual reading of Ps. 119 came to my attention through Stephen G. Dempster, *Dominion and Dynasty: A Theology of the Hebrew Bible* (Downers Grove: IVP, 2003), 200–202.

Jesus quotes Deuteronomy 6:5 with Leviticus 19:18. Loving God and neighbor is the righteous requirement of the law. The thrust of the summary commands orients people away from themselves and toward God and others. The law simultaneously governs a vertical relationship (toward God) and a horizontal relationship (toward neighbor). Every command and condemnation fits within either the vertical or horizontal line of the law (or both). The Ten Commandments basically break down to four commands that specifically govern relationship with God and six directed toward human relationships. Later in the life of Israel, the prophets would condemn the people for two things only: idolatry and injustice. Every sin, transgression, evil act, or thought decried by the prophets will fit under one category or the other.

The Vertical and Horizontal Law

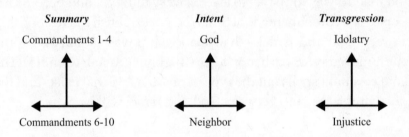

Summary	*Intent*	*Transgression*
Commandments 1-4	God	Idolatry
Commandments 6-10	Neighbor	Injustice

The two directions are of course connected. Love for God is displayed in love for neighbor, and love for neighbor reflects love for God. The law is cast in terms of regulating relationships, which is fitting considering that it was given in a covenantal context. More importantly, the vertical and horizontal relationship planes address the results of the fall and the subsequent curse. The call to love God with your heart, soul, mind, and strength and to love your neighbor as yourself is rooted in ancient intentions and actions. In turn, the great commandments become the focal point of obedience in the new covenant.

105

The Covenant and Redemption

The law was not a legal maze with an "Enter Here" sign at Sinai through which Israel was meant to grope around until the nation found God at the end. The law was given in the context of what was to become *the* biblical pattern of redemption, namely, the exodus. Israel's redemption from Egypt was not dependent on the people's behavior or works; it was 100 percent dependent on God's covenant promise to Abraham. The end of the law was never legalism for righteousness.

God introduced himself to Moses like this: "I am the God of your father, the God of Abraham, the God of Isaac, and the God of Jacob" (Ex. 3:6). All of God's dealings with Israel have to be understood in this light. There is a relationship between God and Israel before Sinai based on God's faithfulness to his promise to Abraham. The law, therefore, was never given as a way to find God but was given after God made a way for Israel to leave slavery in Egypt and become his people. The covenant made at Sinai did not establish the relationship between God and Israel—that relationship was established some four hundred years earlier on a dark night in Canaan (Gen. 15). The Sinai covenant spells out the type of relationship that exists and the way that relationship between God and Israel will work.

God the King and Israel the Subject

There are types of covenants in the Bible that are similar to other ancient Near Eastern practices. The Sinai covenant best fits the pattern of what is called a *suzerain-vassal* treaty. In this type of covenant a greater king (suzerain) promises to protect and provide for a lesser king (vassal), provided the vassal abides by the rules set for the relationship. The suzerain gives protection, and the vassal responds with loyalty and allegiance. Typically the rules of the treaty included things such as tribute of some kind and going to war if called upon. These rules were written down, read aloud, and publically witnessed and confirmed. The basic parts of a suzerain-vassal treaty are present in the narrative of the Sinai covenant.

Covenant Ceremony

• Preamble	Ex. 20:2a
• Historical Prologue	Ex. 20:2b
• Stipulations	Ex. 20:3–17
• Provision for Reading the Covenant	Ex. 24:7
• Witnesses	Ex. 19:8; 24:3, 7
• Blessings and Curses	Ex. 20:5–6
• Oath	Ex. 24:3, 7

What this tells us is that the Israelites would have understood the kind of relationship they had with God and what they were committing to when they said, "All that the LORD has spoken we will do" (19:8). In this covenantal context no one would have viewed the law as the entrance point but as a commitment in accordance with their covenant status established by the Lord God their King.

The Necessity of the Blood. Three specific elements about this ceremony should be noted. For one, the oath attached to the Sinai covenant was sealed in blood. Moses ceremonially cleansed both the altar and the people with blood when the covenant was ratified. The place of sacrifice, where offerings for sin would be made and where God's presence stayed in a special way, was consecrated for maintaining the covenantal relationship. Likewise the people were sprinkled with blood while Moses said: "Behold the blood of the covenant that the LORD has made with you in accordance with all these words" (24:8). This is not the first (nor the last) time in the Bible that a covenant is sealed with blood. The underlying significance of the blood is that it points to the need for sacrifice in order for the people to approach God. Ultimately it illustrates that an obstacle stands in the way between God and the people. He is their God and has redeemed them from Egypt, but they are still unclean. There is a problem that must be fixed, but up to this point in the text a permanent solution has yet to appear; at this point there are only faint lights on the horizon.

Grace and Obedience. The similarities between the Abrahamic and Sinaitic covenants and their ancient Near Eastern

107

counterparts are remarkable. Although the biblical covenants are not exact replicas of other covenants—the two covenants in question, after all, have God as a party—the background does help us to understand the distinctions between the Abrahamic and Sinaitic covenants and the covenantal form of God's redemption.

In the covenant ceremony in Genesis 15, God assumes responsibility to keep the covenant. When he passes between the split animal carcasses, he binds himself to an oath. Note the difference between that ceremony and the one at Sinai. At Sinai the people promise to keep the law. The differences between the Abrahamic and Sinaitic covenants highlight the different emphases found in each covenant.

The covenant that God made with Abraham fits more of a *royal-grant* model, in which a gift, often land, is given without the stipulations found in the Sinai covenant. In a royal-grant covenant a superior party (perhaps a king) might grant the rights to a piece of land to a people group or to a man and his family forever. There are curses involved, but the curses are not laid on the vassal; they are made against any who would try to take the land and ignore the covenant.

The Abrahamic covenant confirms that God *will* keep his promise, and so the emphasis is placed on the unilateral (one-way) nature of the covenant. The Sinaitic covenant, though grounded and steeped in God's redemption of his people and his faithfulness to his word, also stresses the bilateral (two-way) nature of the relationship. The Sinaitic covenant, while clearly displaying God's faithfulness and love for his people, still underscores the necessity of obedience on the part of the people. Two texts summarize the dual emphasis in the narrative.

> **God's Side**: It was not because you were more in number than any other people that the LORD set his love on you and chose you, for you were the fewest of all peoples, but it is because the LORD loves you and is keeping the oath that he swore to your fathers, that the LORD has brought you out with a mighty hand

and redeemed you from the house of slavery, from the hand of Pharaoh king of Egypt. (Deut. 7:7–8)

Israel's Side: And now, O Israel, listen to the statutes and the rules that I am teaching you, and do them, that you may live, and go in and take possession of the land that the LORD, the God of your fathers, is giving you. (Deut. 4:1)

These verses do not imply that righteousness is a joint venture between God and his people (God's grace + Israel's obedience = righteousness) but that it is in keeping with the nature of the kind of covenant relationship between God (the suzerain) and Israel (the vassal). A covenant of this kind fits precisely into the pattern of redemption under construction since Genesis.

Once Again, Genesis 18:17–19. The different emphases found in the two covenants take us back to Genesis 18:17–19. The promise to Abraham is secure; God will keep his word. At the same time, God determines that his word of promise will be kept with *a certain sort of people.* The promise will come to those who do "righteousness and justice" (v. 19). In this way the Sinai covenant, in which "righteousness and justice" are emphasized continually, provides a vision for fulfilling the promise to the Abrahamic covenant. It points Israel to obedience that befits the children of Abraham. The Sinai covenant is not (in any age) heavenly steps for a good life, and far from being a centuries-long time-out for the Abrahamic covenant, it serves the promise and points to that which it takes to fulfill it.

Blessings and Curses. The reward for obedience to the covenant law is life, and the punishment for disobedience is death: "I call heaven and earth to witness against you today, that I have set before you life and death, blessing and curse. Therefore choose life, that you and your offspring may live" (Deut. 30:19). Deuteronomy 28 catalogs the tremendous blessings that will flow from obedience and the horrendous curses for disobedience. These blessings and curses provide the basis for all such words of promise and warning throughout the Bible. Isaiah's image of the future day of blessing (65:15–25) and Jeremiah's prophecy of exile (25:1–11) are based on Deuteronomy 28. The biblical pattern set in Eden—*Obedience = life*; *Disobedience = death*—is set in stone at Sinai.

Out of Egypt I Called My Son

As vital as it is to recognize the covenantal context, we must note that this legalized relationship is also cast in family terms. Just like partnerships or alliances today, ancient Near Eastern covenants were not necessarily based on personal relationships. They were more likely based on practical, military, and/or economic grounds. The Sinai covenant, however much it resembles a suzerain-vassal treaty, is more than that—it is a covenant between Father and son: "Then you shall say to Pharaoh, 'Thus says the LORD, "Israel is my firstborn son, and I say to you, 'Let my son go that he may serve me.' If you refuse to let him go, behold, I will kill your firstborn son."'" (Ex. 4:22–23). The children of Abraham are God's children. This immediately changes the way in which the law works in the community. The people of Israel were not given the legal code of a powerful king from another kingdom to whom they pledged loyalty based on a mutually beneficial relationship; their law came from the God of their fathers, the God who kept his promise to Abraham and rescued them from slavery. He is the God who loves them, provides for them, and protects them—like a father does. Keeping God's law was not just following rules but was obedience to a father by a son.

By keeping the law Israel would be a reflection of its covenant God like a son reflects his father. That is why we hear a refrain like, "You shall be holy because I am holy," and why "I am the LORD your God" is appended to so many stipulations. Through their holiness "they will 'image' God to the nations."[11] Living according to God's law would stir up notice among the nations with the purpose of pointing them to the God of Israel. This is at least one of the reasons God condemns them for their disobedience—it reflects negatively on him and his name. Much later in

11. Dempster, *Dominion and Dynasty*, 101.

Israel's history, as they are suffering under the covenant curses, God declares his reason for acting on their behalf to be "concern for my holy name, which the house of Israel has profaned among the nations" (Ezek. 36:21). Their disobedience belied the righteousness and holiness of God. Parents can relate to such an idea.

The behavior of a child is a source of pride or shame for the parent. My own father once spoke to me like Ezekiel to Judah. The day after a truly remarkable feat of disobedience, he said, "No son of mine should ever behave like that. I raised you different than that, and you know better." By that he did not mean *only* that there were particular, objective rules for our household set by him (suzerain) that I (vassal) was bound to keep; he meant something more than that: as his son, my behavior should reflect well on him, but my disobedience cast a shadow on his name. After all, if the son acts like that, then maybe the father did not do his job. This was not a matter of keeping up appearances, either—it was about honoring him as my father, not putting up a false front but projecting outwardly what he instilled in me. It was my behavior that was false; it belied the reality of my upbringing. That is why he was entirely right to say "you know better." Although all illustrations fall short of capturing the relationship between God and his people, this example captures an aspect of the particular kind of covenant relationship that God has with his people, his children, and the role of obedience.

Obedience as Righteousness

When Moses tells the people that "it will be righteousness for us, if we are careful to do all this commandment before the LORD our God, as he has commanded us" (Deut. 6:25), he connects righteousness directly to obedience. What does it mean to be considered righteous in the Sinai covenant? It means to keep the law. This is not true only in the Sinai covenant because the declaration of righteousness means that everything God desires and wills has been met. Nevertheless, there is an inescapable emphasis on obedience for righteousness in the Sinai covenant.

Through the law God lays out his standard of what it means to live as his children, who are meant to do righteousness and justice.

Recognizing the "do this" emphasis in the law in no way negates faith, for the people of Israel had to believe that God is who he said he is and that he keeps his word and will do all that he promises. For instance, Caleb and Joshua plead with Israel to go into the Promised Land without fear of the Canaanites even though they might be giants. The people, in one of the more psychotic moments in the Old Testament, conclude that the Lord is trying to kill them and decide to stone Caleb and Joshua and return to Egypt (Num. 14:1–10). The Lord intervenes: "And the LORD said to Moses, 'How long will this people despise me? And how long will they not believe in me, in spite of all the signs that I have done among them?'" (v. 11). It is unbelief that fuels their disobedience. Psalm 119 and other texts emphasize the necessity of trusting in God, and there is no doubt that faith is the key to being righteous in God's sight (surely they knew all about Genesis 15), but that does not change the fact that the *emphasis* in the law is "do this and live." In the Sinai covenant faith is always implied, and often explicit, but obedience is always at the forefront. It is, after all, a covenant in which the law figures prominently. It is precisely the prominence of the law in the Sinai covenant that exposes the problem—no one can be justified by doing the works of the law.

Hearts of Flesh, Not Tablets of Stone

There are strong and persistent indicators in the text that there is going to be a real problem if Israel is to attain righteousness through the law. Before reaching the Red Sea the Israelites complain to Moses for bringing them out of Egypt (Ex. 14:10–12). Their fear of Pharaoh's onrushing army is understandable, but their response does not bode well for their future. God saves them and makes his track record with them all the more convincing, but in spite of the growing evidence of God's faithfulness and love, Israel does not improve.

The Ten Commandments are barely minted when we get a glimpse of what to expect in Israel's future (Ex. 32). Before Moses could make it back from Sinai, the people were reveling in a pagan celebration, with a golden calf at the center of the festivities. Aaron, while claiming that the calf just popped out of the fire after he threw the gold in, reminded Moses not to be too surprised: "You know the people, that they are set on evil" (v. 22). In saying this, he echoes God's conclusion given to Moses on Sinai: "I have seen this people, and behold, it is a stiff-necked people" (v. 9).

Increasing Transgressions: The Impact of the Law. From the golden calf fiasco onward, the experience of Israel with the law is never stellar, and there are signs everywhere that something is dreadfully wrong. God relents on behalf of Moses and does not destroy the people after the calf incident, but the relationship between Israel and their covenant God is clearly not the way it ought to be. Rather than making Israel better, the law has the opposite effect on them. Their disobedience receives harsher punishment after Sinai, and their sin continues to mount through various rebellions, nearly constant grumbling, and even worshiping Baal and mixing with women from the very nations before whom they were meant to display the glory of the Lord.[12] In short, "Sinai does something profoundly negative to Israel."[13]

Reconciliation at a Distance. Besides outright disobedience and rebellion, there are signs both before and after the law is given that show how life under the Sinaitic law is not going to produce the righteousness that leads to life. When Moses and the elders go up Sinai, the elders have to stay at a distance, and God warns Moses not to let the people touch the edge of the mountain (Ex. 19:12). The people are happy to oblige. This is understandable given the smoke, lightning, and thunder (although Moses does tell them not to be afraid—20:20), but there is something wrong when

12. The incident with the Israelite and the Midianite woman, which Phinehas addressed with his spear, is an example.
13. Dempster, *Dominion and Dynasty*, 112. This section is influenced almost entirely by Dempster's discussion, 112–13.

the God who declares himself to be their God and they his people must warn them to keep their distance lest he "break out against them" (19:24). There is space between God and the people—even at the best of times. The giving of the law itself is an example of the space between God and the people because although they do have God's righteous law revealed to them, they receive it only through Moses' mediation. This is not the reconciliation that Paul describes in Romans 5:1–11.

The Problem according to Moses. In addition to the exodus and Sinai narratives that give ample proof of whether the people will be right with God on the basis of doing the law, there are also explicit statements. When recounting the bleak history of the wilderness wanderings, Moses asks:

> And now, Israel, what does the LORD your God require of you, but to fear the LORD your God, to walk in all his ways, to love him, to serve the LORD your God with all your heart and with all your soul, and to keep the commandments and statutes of the LORD, which I am commanding you today for your good? (Deut. 10:12–13)

Without a deep change, however, they will not do these things. Moses speaks a word to them that will echo down through Scripture, through the prophets and into a promise of a new kind of relationship: "Circumcise therefore the foreskin of your heart, and be no longer stubborn" (v. 16). Moses exposes the fact that this is not just a law problem but a heart problem. In doing so Moses reveals the true meaning of circumcision. The law presents God's righteous standards and shows what it takes to attain righteousness, but the problem is that the law does not give the thing needed to keep it—a new heart.[14] Apart from a new heart, it is clear from reading the narrative that there is "a hermeneutic that points to the failure of Israel to keep the Sinai covenant and to

14. See James M. Hamilton's discussion of Israel's "heart problem" in *God's Salvation through Judgment: A Biblical Theology* (Wheaton, IL: Crossway, 2010), 123–25.

the virtual inevitability of exile on these terms."[15] The curse of exile appears unavoidable. Moses says as much in Deuteronomy 4 when he tells the people that they will not live long in the Promised Land and that "the LORD will scatter you among the peoples, and you will be left few in number among the nations where the LORD will drive you" (v. 27).

The Problem according to the Prophets. The prophets confirm what the historical narratives show so well: the nation did not improve over time but became worse.

> But this command I gave them: "Obey my voice, and I will be your God, and you shall be my people. And walk in all the way that I command you, that it may be well with you."
>
> But they did not obey or incline their ear, but walked in their own counsels and the stubbornness of their evil hearts, and went backward and not forward. From the day that your fathers came out of the land of Egypt to this day, I have persistently sent all my servants the prophets to them, day after day. Yet they did not listen to me or incline their ear, but stiffened their neck. They did worse than their fathers. (Jer. 7:23–26)

The prophets take up Moses' heart-circumcision image to draw a distinction between keeping the law by rote (particularly the sacrifices) and keeping the law out of devotion to God. Through Isaiah, God decries the hypocrisy that passed for worship among people who "draw near with their mouth and honor me with their lips, while their hearts are far from me" (Isa. 29:13). Going through the motions was not all that difficult for many in Israel, and their pseudo law-keeping stirred God's anger, as clearly heard in his rejection of their sacrifices and customs.

> "What to me is the multitude of your sacrifices?" says the LORD; "I have had enough of burnt offerings of rams and the fat of well-fed beasts; I do not delight in the blood of bulls, or of lambs, or of goats." (1:11)

15. Dempster, *Dominion and Dynasty*, 113.

Over and again the prophets condemn Israel's empty, hypocritical rituals (e.g., Jer. 6:20; Amos 5:22) and the injustice carried out on fellow covenant citizens (e.g., Isa. 5:23; Amos 5:11–12)—again, a failure to love God and neighbor. Amos even says that through their sacrifices they "multiply transgression" (4:4). The tendencies of the exodus generation were manifested in their children, who because of the "stubbornness of their evil hearts" managed to outdo their ancestors in spite of God's continual patience (Jer. 7:23–26). Instead of doing righteousness and justice, they "turn justice to wormwood and cast down righteousness to the earth!" (Amos 5:7). Like Moses, the prophets declare that the righteousness God requires cannot be attained unless there is a drastic change in the heart, which is exactly what God will supply.

They Will All Know God. Although several texts in the Prophets look forward to a new day when God will act on behalf of his people, two in particular address the heart problem that cripples Israel. Through Jeremiah, God promises a new covenant: "I will put my law within them, and I will write it on their hearts. And I will be their God, and they shall be my people" (Jer. 31:33). The standard of God's righteousness will be engraved on human hearts rather than in a set of external statutes and ordinances. The law in the heart is coupled with an intimate knowledge of God—"they shall all know me, from the least of them to the greatest" (v. 34)—and underscores the point made earlier that obedience cannot be separated from loyalty to the Lawgiver. The idea is picked up in the next chapter as Jeremiah prophesies the end of the Babylonian exile and the great work that God will do in his people.

> I will give them one heart and one way, that they may fear me forever, for their own good and the good of their children after them. I will make with them an everlasting covenant, that I will not turn away from doing good to them. And I will put the fear of me in their hearts, that they may not turn from me. I will rejoice in doing them good, and I will plant them in this land in faithfulness, with all my heart and all my soul. (32:39–41)

The law exposed the need that God provides. In Deuteronomy, God promises blessings for obedience, and here in Jeremiah he promises to give them the very thing needed for obedience—hearts wholly devoted to him. So God gives the means for obedience and then pours out his greatest blessing, eternal love for his children and heart-and-soul faithfulness. Surely there is an echo of the Shema: "love the LORD your God with all your heart and with all your soul and with all your might," except here it is God's love for his people rather than theirs for him.

The future foreseen by Jeremiah is also prophesied by Ezekiel, through whom God also promises an end to exile (the curse of law-breaking) and a new life of Spirit-driven obedience:

> I will sprinkle clean water on you, and you shall be clean from all your uncleannesses, and from all your idols I will cleanse you. And I will give you a new heart, and a new spirit I will put within you. And I will remove the heart of stone from your flesh and give you a heart of flesh. And I will put my Spirit within you, and cause you to walk in my statutes and be careful to obey my rules. (36:25–27)

The righteous standard of the law will be fulfilled by people who have God's Spirit. To put it another way, God himself will do a work in the hearts of his people to make them righteous (see Deut. 30:6). In Ezekiel 37 there is the famous vision of the dry bones that come to life, a prophecy of the Spirit's coming upon God's people. The result is that they will "know that I am the LORD" (vv. 13–14). Jeremiah and Ezekiel both look forward to a day when God will make for himself children of Abraham who do "justice and righteousness" and so fulfill the promise spoken to Abraham.

God wills his unconditional promise to Abraham to be fulfilled through a particular kind of people, so he does everything necessary to fulfill his promise—including taking away the sin barrier that prevents obedience. Both Jeremiah and Ezekiel connect the promise of a new heart with the forgiveness of sins. A new heart will be possible because "I will forgive their iniquity, and I will remember their sin no more" (Jer. 31:34), and he will "cleanse you from all your iniquities" (Ezek. 36:33). The sin problem, which predates Sinai by centuries, could not, nor was it meant to be, solved by the law. The law, like the covenant to which it is attached, points to the solution to the Adam problem.

Conclusion

The Servant of Yahweh: Justification through the True Israel

Isaiah looks forward to the coming of One who will take up the role of Israel. The Servant of God will accomplish everything necessary for people to be made right with God and will bring the promises of God to their appointed fulfillment. With his coming there will be justice for the nations (Isa. 42:1). He will be given as "a covenant for the people" and "a light for the nations" (v. 6). Because of him, God's Spirit will be poured out on coming generations (44:3) and God will be glorified in him (49:3). Through this Righteous One many will be accounted righteous (53:11) on the basis of his atoning suffering and death. Isaiah's Servant is set in the context of the historical disobedience (idolatry and injustice) of Israel. The Servant will live according to the will of God and complete his work, vindicating God's name and redeeming God's people from exile. This is where the Sinai covenant was headed all along.

The Law and the Flow of Redemption

According to Paul, the law serves many purposes, but none of them as important as the main goal of bringing forward the promise made to Abraham. It both serves the promise and leads us to Christ, the fulfillment of the promise. Through the curse of the law the promise to Abraham was fulfilled and the blessing flowed to the nations.

Christ redeemed us from the curse of the law by becoming a curse for us—for it is written, "Cursed is everyone who is hanged on a tree"—so that in Christ Jesus the blessing of Abraham might come to the Gentiles, so that we might receive the promised Spirit through faith. (Gal. 3:13–14)

The Sinai covenant is something like a pipeline in the Bible. It is a conduit through which the promise made to Abraham flows to its fulfillment in Christ.

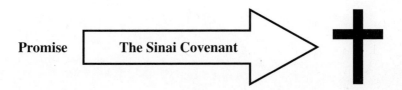

Promise. The curse of the law is death for disobedience—again, just as it was for Adam. The law provides the concrete basis for the judgment of sin, and unless the curse for disobedience is overturned, there can be no salvation. But the righteousness of God, witnessed in the law and revealed in Christ, is the answer to the curse, an answer to Adam, an answer to the law, and the fulfillment of the promise to Abraham. With that in mind, it is now time to turn our attention to the New Testament teaching on justification by faith in Christ.

6

God's Righteousness
and Ours

Far better news the gospel brings:
It bids us fly and gives us wings.[1]

CHAPTER 5 DEALT WITH the old covenant law and how it was not designed to provide the righteousness demanded in it. That righteousness must come from God himself, as he promised from Deuteronomy to the Prophets. This chapter focuses on some of the main New Testament texts that establish the fulfillment of God's promise of righteousness in Christ.

- God's Righteousness: Who God Is and What God Does
- Romans 10:3–6
- Philippians 3:1–9
- Sharing in Christ, the Righteousness of God: Union and Justification
- 2 Corinthians 5:21
- 1 Corinthians 1:30
- Conclusion

1. This is the second half of the quote (see the beginning of chapter 5) often attributed to John Bunyan.

God's Righteousness: Who God Is and What God Does

The meaning of the phrase *the righteousness of God* is central to the doctrine of justification. The three major interpretations are: (1) God's judging and saving action in Christ through which the believer is legally declared to be righteous as a gift through faith in Christ; (2) God's saving act on the basis of Christ's death and resurrection in which the declaration of righteousness includes an effective transformation of the believer through the power of the Spirit; or (3) God's covenantal faithfulness displayed in the cross of Christ, the ultimate fulfillment of his promise to Abraham.

At times it is hard to distinguish among the views since there is unavoidable overlap in both texts and terminology, and because the search for a nice and tidy definition for something like the righteousness of God can be elusive. It is difficult these days to say, "I think the righteousness of God is (fill in the blank)" and not hear back, "Yes, but . . ."—even from those who agree with you.

If the views above seem to overlap at points, it is because they *do* overlap—at least at points. Although I believe that one view is the primary way in which the Bible speaks of God's righteousness, I do not reject the other views as having no basis in Scripture. I see them as subordinate but not wrong. The righteousness of God is comprehensive, connecting to every aspect of salvation, and varied, receiving different emphases at points in Scripture.[2]

The Faithfulness of God

The righteousness of God includes his faithfulness to his promises. God's righteousness as his faithfulness to keep his word is also quite often connected to salvation. Zechariah 8 speaks of a day when God, in fulfillment of his promises, will establish in Zion his people, a remnant who will live in joy and peace in the presence of God. He declares:

2. See Michael F. Bird, *Introducing Paul: The Man, His Mission and His Message* (Downers Grove, IL: IVP, 2008), 93–95.

> Behold, I will save my people from the east country and from
> the west country, and I will bring them to dwell in the midst
> of Jerusalem. And they shall be my people, and I will be their
> God, in faithfulness and in righteousness. (vv. 7–8)

Although faithfulness and righteousness are identical in this text,
the display of God's righteousness goes hand in hand with his
faithfulness and salvation. This view of God's righteousness also
corresponds with his judgment of the nations (9:1–7). The promise of blessing to the nations is in view as well, for in the larger
context even some former enemies from the nations will come
to Jerusalem to worship the Lord (14:16). Nevertheless, this text,
like other Old Testament texts cited in support of this view, does
not establish that God's righteousness *is* his covenant faithfulness, or that it is a synonym for salvation.[3] God's faithfulness to
his promises is part and parcel of the salvation of Israel and the
nations through the covenant with Abraham, but that salvation is
itself *part* of God's plan for creation—the larger context in which
God's covenant promises are contained.

In Romans 3:3–7, Paul connects God's righteousness to
his faithfulness to Israel in spite of Israel's unfaithfulness and
unrighteousness. Yet even here Paul's big idea is not to establish the righteousness of God *as defined by* his covenantal righteousness but to show that God is completely within his rights
in condemning the world, both Jew and Gentile, for sin.[4] Again,
there is a larger context that overshadows covenantal faithfulness, namely God's rights as Creator to judge the world. The world
(Jew and Gentile and creation itself), as Paul makes crystal clear
in Romans, is dead in Adam, with the curse permeating every
layer of existence. Moreover, since the closing of Eden, God has
a charge of rebellion lodged against Adam and his children, and
that charge must be addressed. In the larger picture of the Bible,
and before Abraham, the promise of a victorious seed from Eve

---

3. Examples include Pss. 36:10; 71:2; 98:2; Isa. 51:5.
4. Stephen Westerholm, *Perspectives Old and New on Paul: The "Lutheran" Paul and His Critics* (Grand Rapids: Eerdmans, 2004), 292–93.

(Gen. 3:15) impels salvation. God's covenantal faithfulness to Abraham is a manifestation of his larger program of redemption of the world. When we speak of God's righteousness, we should not exclude his faithfulness to keep his promises, but if we define his righteousness as his covenantal faithfulness, then we have said too little.

The Transforming Power of God

It is also evident that God's power to save and transform is linked to his righteousness. Paul speaks of the gospel as "the power of God for salvation" (Rom. 1:16). Later he says, "the righteousness of God has been manifested" (3:21) in his saving action in the sacrifice of Christ. Many see a dual emphasis on the *activity* of God to bring about not only a new status (justified) but also the power for a new life of obedience. Sharing in both Christ's death and resurrection, believers have "been set free from sin" (6:7, 18). They are no longer enslaved to sin but free to pursue righteous obedience (vv. 11–13). In another place Paul connects the righteousness of God to the new creation that believers become through faith in Christ (2 Cor. 5:17–21). Too often justification declared upon faith and the new life of the justified (often described as justification and sanctification) are practically severed and we fail to see them flowing inseparably together. The legal declaration should not be blurred into the transformation that takes place in the believer through the Spirit.

A good example of how the work of the Spirit is connected yet distinct from other aspects of salvation is found in Titus 3:4–7. Here Paul speaks of salvation's being grounded in God's mercy and applied by the Spirit that comes to us through Jesus (vv. 5–6), so that those who are justified would be the heirs of eternal life (v. 7). No one should argue that regeneration and justification are independent actions to the extent that one could be regenerated while awaiting justification (or vice versa) in some sort of chronological way, but Paul does not make them identical. God's righteousness in declaring a sinner to be just through Christ is

124

not the same thing as the renewal by the Spirit. Fully integrated, to be certain, but distinct nonetheless.

Judging and Saving Righteousness

God's saving action in Christ, through whom sinners are declared to be legally just, combines his judgment against sin and his free gift of salvation. On the surface the two ideas seem to be polar opposites—but as the pattern of redemption in the Bible since the exodus shows, the two strands are woven so tightly together that they make one cord.

God upheld his justice against the sin of rebellion by providing Christ as the sacrifice of atonement—"a propitiation by his blood" (Rom. 3:25). The word *propitiation* points to the sacrifice of Christ as that which turns away God's just anger against sin. The Greek word (*hilastērion*) is used for the mercy seat that covered the ark of the covenant in the temple (Lev. 16:2, 13–15). On the Day of Atonement, the priest would sprinkle blood from the sacrifice on the mercy seat to atone for sin. So here Paul calls Christ's death on the cross a propitiation, signifying that Jesus is the place where sacrifice is made to turn away God's wrath. It is not, however, just the *place* of sacrifice in view here but also the sacrifice itself—the cross of Christ represents both place and thing; as Paul puts it, God "put *him* forward as a *propitiation* in his blood."

God's wrath against sin is central to Paul's discussion that begins in Romans 3:18, and here the question of God's just exercise of his wrath and the question of God's salvation come together in one answer: God pours out his wrath on Christ, our mercy seat and sacrificial substitute who bears the full weight of our sin.[5] God's justice and mercy meet at the cross. As Paul says, God did this "to show *his righteousness* at the present time, so that he might be just and the justifier of the one who has faith in Jesus" (Rom. 3:26).

---

5. At the cross, the great eschatological day of God's wrath breaks into the present. The prophets contain many references to that day (e.g., Isa. 13:9, 13; Ezek. 7:19; 38:18–19; Zeph. 1:15, 18).

125

God's righteousness requires sin to be punished, and he is absolutely right to do so because the whole world is accountable to him for their unrighteousness. God's righteousness is exercised and vindicated in the sacrifice of Christ and expressed in judging and saving through Christ as a gift to sinners justified by faith.[6] This view best captures the righteousness of God as revealed in the Bible. The Bible also has quite a bit to say about how the righteousness of God is applied in justification, how it contrasts with our own works-driven righteousness, and how God's righteousness becomes ours in Christ. The rest of this chapter deals with some of the main texts in Paul associated with righteousness and justification.

Romans 10:3–6

The righteousness of God, displayed in Christ and his cross, is the righteousness that Paul in Romans 10:3 accuses the Jews of not knowing: "For, being ignorant of the righteousness that comes from God, and seeking to establish their own, they did not submit to God's righteousness." What was the righteousness that they tried to establish? By missing the ultimate intent and purpose of the law, many in Israel pursued a performance-based righteousness through the law. Their so-called zeal for God— examples of which are the crucifixion of Christ and later Paul's persecution of the church—was not just misplaced or in need of adjustment but not "according to knowledge." By rejecting Christ, the goal of the law "for righteousness to everyone who believes" (v. 4), they rejected the Lawgiver.

This text is historically (notoriously?) difficult to understand, not only because of verse 4 but also because of Paul's quote and interpretation of Deuteronomy 30:12–14 (Rom. 10:6–8) that follows on the heels of his quote of Leviticus 18:5

---

6. Westerholm, *Perspectives*, 285, sums up the righteousness of God as "that salvific activity by which God's commitment to uphold the right is vindicated at the same time as sinners (those guilty of *un*dikaiosness of Rom. 1:18) who believe the gospel become *dikaios*."

(Rom. 10:5). A tension within the law itself seems to arise, with Leviticus emphasizing righteousness through doing the commandments and Deuteronomy establishing faith-based law-keeping.

Leviticus 18:5	Deuteronomy 30:12–14
For Moses writes about the righteousness that is based on the law, that the person who does the commandments shall live by them. (Rom. 10:5)	But the righteousness based on faith says, "Do not say in your heart, 'Who will ascend into heaven?' (that is, to bring Christ down) or 'Who will descend into the abyss?'(that is, to bring Christ up from the dead)." But what does it say? "The word is near you, in your mouth and in your heart." (Rom. 10:6–8)

A contrast between doing and believing is established in Romans 9:30–33, where Paul pits righteousness through faith attained by the Gentiles against the failure of the Jews to attain righteousness through law-keeping. When Paul says they did not "pursue" the law by faith, he is speaking specifically about their inability to discern where the law was leading them. Ultimately, Paul is not condemning Jews for trying to keep the law—the commands, after all, were meant to be kept—but for trying to both maintain and attain righteousness on the basis of their works rather than righteousness through faith in Christ, the fulfillment of the law. That is why Paul connects what he says in 9:30–32 to a combined quote of Isaiah 8:14 and 28:16: "They have stumbled over the stumbling stone, as it is written, 'Behold, I am laying in Zion a stone of stumbling, and a rock of offense; and whoever believes in him will not be put to shame'" (Rom. 9:32–33). In trying to establish their own righteousness based on doing the law, they stumbled over the Messiah; they failed to believe in God's appointed purpose and aim of the law. In their pursuit of righteousness based on works, they missed Christ, the "overall, long-term aim of the law."[7]

Christ in the Law

This Christ-centered understanding of the law lies behind Paul's use of Leviticus 18 and Deuteronomy 30. Deuteronomy 30:12–14 comes right after the section that outlines the blessings and curses for either obedience or disobedience of God. Paul capitalizes on the future orientation of Deuteronomy 30, in which a return from exile (vv. 1–2) sets the scene for the rest of the chapter. Moses speaks of a time *after* the curses for disobedience—exile—are over. The outlook is bleak—Israel will fail to obey and will be sent into exile—but the future is filled with the hope of a day when "the LORD your God will circumcise your heart and the heart of your offspring, so that you will love the LORD your God with all your heart and with all your soul, that you may live" (v. 6). Although the law was "not too hard" nor "far off" but "very near" (vv. 11, 14), it would not be kept by Israel but would be fulfilled in Christ. This is why Paul interprets "ascend into heaven" as "bring Christ down," and "descend into the abyss" as "bring Christ up from the dead." The near "word" is the word of the gospel—the one way of righteousness promised in the law. The righteousness based on the law (Lev. 18:5) will not be attained by *doing* but by believing in Christ. This understanding fits the idea, mentioned earlier, that the main goal of the Sinai covenant in general, which necessarily included the covenant law, was to bring the promise forward to its fulfillment in Christ in order to provide an objective, public basis for judgment (Rom. 3:20; Gal. 3:13–14) and so lead to the gospel's going to the nations. The righteousness of God is attained only through faith in Christ.

7. John Piper, *The Future of Justification: A Response to N. T. Wright* (Wheaton, IL: Crossway, 2007), 193. Piper argues convincingly for his christological interpretation of Rom. 9:30–10:4 in "Appendix One," 191–95. Also see the excellent discussion in Jason C. Meyer, *The End of the Law: Mosaic Covenant in Pauline Theology* (Nashville: B&H, 2009), 209–29.

Philippians 3:1–9

In Philippians 3, Paul draws a clear line in the sand between works righteousness and righteousness as a gift from God through faith in Christ.[8] In Paul's sights are Judaizers—Jews who claimed to believe in Christ but who held to certain aspects of the law as essential for salvation. At the top of their righteousness to-do list was circumcision for Gentile believers. Perhaps it sounded something like this: "Yes you need Jesus, we all agree on that, but what you need is Jesus *and* circumcision." The "Jesus *and* . . ." syndrome will be dealt with later in this book, but for now it is enough to say that holding to anything in addition to Christ for righteousness is to call God a liar and to trust in ourselves.

What Is Works Righteousness?

It is often said that there was no works righteousness among first-century Jews (and thus among Jewish believers), at least not in the sense of trying to do something by which they hoped to earn God's favor. The problem that Paul and the early church faced, so it is said, is that the Jewish believers were excluding Gentiles from equal covenant status. As Jews they believed in grace and were a part of the covenant already, so therefore had no need to earn a place before God. Therefore, the argument goes, there was no idea of earning righteousness. Their sin was not works righteousness but ethnic exclusion of the Gentiles from the people of God. Clearly there was a drive for the Gentile Christians to be circumcised and to adhere, to whatever extent, to the law, but there was more going on than that. There was a near-total misunderstanding on the part of many first-century Jews as to what amounted to righteousness before God. The gospel made God's standard as clear as the midday sun, but to the Judaizers, or the circumcision party, as to unbelieving Jews in that day, it was still 4:00 A.M.

---

8. Unlike many interpreters, I do not see the big issue here as a matter of a shift in salvation history (though clearly that happened) but a clash between righteousness by works and righteousness by grace through faith.

When the gospel is proclaimed, when the declaration goes out that the goal of the law has been reached because God has acted once and for all by fulfilling all his promises and providing a way for the ultimate forgiveness of sins, and then you turn around and demand circumcision or some other law-keeping, you are not just denying some people entrance into the covenant community (though that is absolutely happening), you are establishing your own way of what it means to be righteous. *Even if* the problem *could* be summed up by saying that they had failed to see what, in the light of Christ, it means to be the people of God, it would still be a matter of establishing the basis of one's status before God on some grounds other than what God had proclaimed to be true in Christ Jesus. If it looks like a duck and works like a duck, it is a works-righteousness duck.

The question is, what do we mean by works righteousness? I take it to mean an attempt to establish righteousness in any way other than how God intends.[9] So if God has established that Gentiles are part of his people through faith in Christ, and the Judaizers are saying, "No, you have to get circumcised," then they are establishing their own basis for what it means to be righteous. As Paul would say, they are putting confidence in the flesh (Phil. 3:3–4). God says one thing; they say another. God says believe the gospel; they say, "Yes, but also keep the law." Slice it whatever way you please, that is works righteousness.

Law Righteousness versus Gift Righteousness

In Philippians 3, Paul contrasts two kinds of righteousness.[10] Whatever his past achievements and accomplishments, what he used to count as assets he now sees as liabilities.[11] If the Judaizers

9. I make the same observations regarding N. T. Wright and James Dunn's interpretations of Rom. 9:30–10:4 in *Jesus' Blood and Righteousness: Paul's Theology of Imputation* (Wheaton, IL: Crossway, 2006), 121n47.

10. I use the phrase *two kinds of righteousness* and similar phrases here and other places. The phrase, and the content behind it (which permeates this book), is from Martin Luther, "Two Kinds of Righteousness," in *Martin Luther's Basic Theological Writings*, ed. Timothy F. Lull (Minneapolis: Fortress, 1989), 155–64.

11. Moisés Silva, *Philippians*, 2nd ed., Baker Exegetical Commentary on the New Testament (Grand Rapids: Baker, 2005), 157.

think they have reason to boast in their achievements, they have nothing on Paul. He was a Jew through and through. He could trace his family heritage; he was conservative, a follower of the traditions, and a Pharisee (v. 5). He then adds two things that often cause interpreters problems. His zealousness was evident in his persecution of the church, and he was "as to righteousness under the law, blameless" (v. 6). Paul lists things that he came to by birth and background, and then he adds to those his own accomplishments.

Think of Paul's description of his accomplishments as something like the prayer of the Pharisee in the parable of Luke 18.[12] The Pharisee thanks God that he is not a sinner like the tax collector and goes on to display the feathers in his cap. He rests on his own righteousness. Paul acknowledges what he has by virtue of birth and blessing, and then moves on to his own achievements. The Pharisee's thankfulness to God is hollow, given his posturing and his list of overly pious achievements. Paul's persecution of the church destroys any cultural and ethnic distinctions in which he might have rested and, more importantly, belies his blameless law-keeping. Like the Pharisee in the parable, Paul never went home justified—not until he came to believe in the righteousness that God gives in Christ.

Rejecting God and Keeping the Law

In the way the hymn writer John Newton never forgot his former life as a slave trader, so Paul's past persecution seems frequently to have been on his mind (cf. Gal. 1:13). As made clear to him on the road to Damascus, his conversion (not an awakening or realignment) experience narrated in Acts 9, the real object of his persecution was Christ (Acts 9:4). Was Paul well-intentioned at the time? Did he believe that he had God's best interests in mind? Did he think that he was protecting his beloved heritage

---

12. This illustration came to mind after reading a comment in Peter T. O'Brien, *Commentary on Philippians*, NIGTC (Grand Rapids: Eerdmans, 1991), 395–96, about observations made by Robert Gundry in "Grace, Works, and Staying Saved in Paul," *Biblica* 66 (1985): 1–38.

and law? Yes, without a doubt, to all three questions. Of course the same could be said of the Pharisees and scribes who aligned themselves against Jesus, regardless of however many personal/national interests were involved. Who did they reject, persecute, and finally kill? God incarnate. Yet they were driven by a zeal for the law and their traditions.

Like those who crucified Jesus, "the sons of those who murdered the prophets" (Matt. 23:31), Paul knew the law but did not know God. If he had, he would not have persecuted the followers of the One to whom the law pointed. If Paul was a faithful member of the covenant, then so were the people whom Jesus addressed as vipers and whitewashed tombs and who accused him of being in league with Satan. In that case the Jews who conspired to kill Jesus as a blasphemer, as one who deserved to be cursed and killed like the rebellious, gluttonous, drunken son of Deuteronomy 21:18–21 (Matt. 11:19; cf. Luke 7:34), were also faithful to God and the covenant since they believed that they were upholding both. If it is possible to be a member of the covenant, resting in God's grace, *and* to oppose violently what God is doing in the world, then both the Pharisees and Paul were shining examples of covenantal faithfulness and love for their covenant God.

Paul's Blamelessness. When Paul says he was "blameless" with regard to the law, he is not talking about perfection the way we sometimes speak of sinless perfection but of living according to the rules/standards of the law in a regular and observable way. He followed the commandments and kept the sacrifices. He could point to his law-keeping and say, "See, I do what it says." On that level he had a kind of righteousness, but like his zeal, it was not according to knowledge. He did not know God. If he had known God, he would have been like Simeon and welcomed the long-expected Messiah (Luke 2:25–35). But as it happened, when confronted by what God was doing in Christ, Paul decided that the thing to do was to stop it. It comes down to this: *One cannot truly claim to keep the law or to be a faithful member of the covenant and simultaneously persecute the people of God—whether one of the Old Testament prophets, Jesus, or the New Testament church!*

It is not the case that Paul was formerly a faithful member of the covenant community loyal to God but was now directed on a better way only hinted at before, or that God had opened his eyes to see that a new chapter in the history of redemption had begun; Paul's blamelessness before the law was no different from the law righteousness for which he condemns his fellow Jews in Romans 9:32.[13] Whatever his blamelessness amounted to, it did not amount to God's standard of righteousness through faith in Christ, the goal of the law, alone.

A Righteousness Not of My Own

The "righteousness of my own that comes from the law" is Paul's own righteousness and is set over against "the righteousness from God." The two kinds of righteousness in Philippians 3:9 distinguish true God-given righteousness from false, personally generated righteousness. It is not all that complicated to understand what Paul means by "my own." For a start, there is his list in verses 4–6, although his law righteousness was not limited to those things. He refers to all his efforts at righteousness through the law which, as we have seen, was never able nor meant to provide the full status of righteousness before God. It is Paul's efforts versus God's gift. In both cases righteousness is the end point—but only one path leads there. There is a righteousness that comes as a result of doing the law, and there is a righteousness that comes from God through faith in Christ. One is God's righteousness; the other is our own.

The righteousness from the law is Paul's own, but the righteousness from God is through faith. Although "work/s" is not used here explicitly, the contrast between faith and works (cf. Rom. 4:1–8) is right beneath the surface. That conclusion, however, depends at least in part on how we read a phrase found in verse 9. The Greek phrase (*dia pisteōs Christou*) can be read as

13. My view of Paul's pre-Christian life/status differs substantially from N. T. Wright's (and many others'). See his discussion of this text in *Justification: God's Plan & Paul's Vision* (Downers Grove: IVP, 2009), 144–49.

Christ's being the object of ("through faith in Christ," as in RSV, ESV, NASB) or the subject of faith ("through the faithfulness of Christ" or "through Christ's faithfulness"). It is a question of how to read the phrase in Greek usage historically and contextually. Acknowledging the good arguments to the contrary, I take the phrase here to mean "faith *in* Christ," because Paul has been talking about the personal righteousness identified in his background and evidenced in his actions in regard to righteousness, and then denies that way of righteousness in favor of believing in Christ. Again, the parallel is Romans 4:1–8. Ultimately, it seems to me that "faith in Christ" fits best with the next phrase, which explains that the righteousness is "from God on the basis of faith" (NASB). It is faith in Christ (object of faith) that both replaces and also kills the motivation to attain a righteous standing before God through works.

Sharing in Christ, the Righteousness of God: Union and Justification

The life promised in the law could not be achieved through the law but is available through the resurrection of Christ. Here the vital concept of union with Christ comes to the forefront. There are many things to say about union, but one way to think of it is like an umbrella. Union with Christ overarches the grand story of redemption. Election (Eph. 1:3–4), death (1 Thess. 4:14), resurrection and glorification (1 Cor. 15:22), new creation (2 Cor. 5:17), and obedience (Rom. 6:4) are all in union with Christ.[14] In Philippians 3:9, as in other places (e.g., 2 Cor. 5:21) where righteousness language is featured, union with Christ as a legal union is primary.

Here is how having a legal, sometimes called *forensic*, union with Christ works: in God's court of law we stand accused of high treason. The standard by which we are judged is clear

14. John Murray, *Redemption Accomplished and Applied* (Grand Rapids: Eerdmans, 1955), 162–64. Although some may consider it dated, Murray's book deserves a place on the shelf of every pastor and student of the Bible.

(Rom. 3:19–20), and the evidence against us is overwhelming (vv. 10–18). The verdict is handed down: *guilty*. The sentence is death. God, being righteous, carries out the sentence, and his justified wrath against sin is poured out like "a cup of horror and desolation" (Ezek. 23:33). The cup of wrath, however, is swallowed by one in our place, one who is "crushed for our iniquities" (Isa. 53:5). In Christ we died (Rom. 6:3–4), and God deems that Christ's death is truly and legally our death. But God, being righteous and faithful to his word, declares: "I have taken from your hand the cup of staggering; the bowl of my wrath you shall drink no more" (Isa. 51:22). Christ, having carried our sin and guilt, defeats death and is raised from the grave, and his resurrection becomes our resurrection; his life, our life (1 Cor. 15:22). Now, through faith, God sees us only in and through his Son, and God declares us not guilty. If it is true of Christ, it is true of us. Of course, this does not include his deity or divine attributes, but insofar as God accepts Christ's obedient life and substitutionary death for sin—his acceptance being evidenced in the resurrection—so he fully accepts us not only as pardoned but as those who in Christ have "the righteousness of God that depends on faith." So in Philippians 3, when Paul says he wants to be "found in" Christ, he is speaking of this kind of union.

"Alien" Righteousness through Union with Christ

The righteousness that we have before God in Christ is Christ's righteousness and not ours in any independent sense. Historically this is referred to as *alien* righteousness. In a post-*Star Wars* and *E. T.* world, this language can sound a little strange. In the past, *alien* did not refer to extraterrestrial creatures but to something outside us or something not inherent in us. The righteousness that comes to us as a gift from God through the faith that unites us to Christ remains Christ's righteousness. The righteousness in view is not our righteousness, as though God has transferred a certain amount of righteousness to us like a commodity or something that can be quantified in a point system. We have Christ himself and all his benefits of a perfect life and his death and resurrection on our behalf.

2 Corinthians 5:21: Becoming the Righteousness of God in Christ

Another important union text directly connected to justification/righteousness is 2 Corinthians 5:21: "For our sake he made him to be sin who knew no sin, so that in him we might become the righteousness of God." As noted earlier, "made him to be sin" refers to Christ's becoming a sacrifice for our sin.[15] Our sin and guilt are laid on Christ, who suffers the punishment of death that we deserved. In Christ our sin is exchanged for his righteousness. Here Paul sums up the content of his ministry of reconciliation—through God's judging and saving work in Christ (his righteousness), believers in union with Christ share in his death (vv. 14–15), and because of that God does not count our sins against us (v. 19) but makes the believer a "new creation" in Christ (v. 17). The corporate nature of justification is evident in this text. By *corporate*, what is meant is that we share in Christ's death and resurrection as though we ourselves died and rose to new life. He is our representative before God, and what is his, and what he has done, becomes truly and fully ours in him.

Christ the Second Adam

When Paul says that "we . . . become the righteousness of God," he is saying that we become the embodiment, the manifestation, of God's action in Christ. God counts our sin to Christ and counts his righteousness to us. Even though the language is different from that in Romans 4:1–8 and 5:18–19, the idea of the imputation of Christ's righteousness and the imputation of our sin to him undergirds this text. Like Romans 4, Paul places

15. I argue in detail for an Old Testament sacrificial background for this text in *Jesus' Blood and Righteousness*, 160–70.

136

the emphasis here on the forgiveness of sins rather than on the positive counting of Christ's obedience. However, we should note that the idea of life as a result of Christ's work is present in 2 Corinthians 5:17, where Paul speaks of becoming a "new creation." The themes of representation, life, and righteousness combined in this text point to Paul's theology of Christ as the second Adam.

> Though not explicitly stated as in Romans 5 or 1 Corinthians 15, Christ's role as the second Adam is in view. Support for this interpretation exists not only in the similarity with Paul's more explicit Adam/Christ texts, it is found in the context as well. Just as Adam was head of the original creation and his act affected the status of those who followed, so the act of Christ (i.e., death for sin [vv. 14, 19, 21]) affects the status of those who follow him. His death "for all" leads to their becoming a "new creation" in him. Christ's representative death, moreover, has real results for those for whom he died. The purpose . . . of his death "for all" was to bring about a new life that is lived for Christ rather than living, as previously, for themselves (v. 15, "they who live might no longer . . . live for themselves"). Just as Adam's act of sin led to a life of sin and death for those who followed, so Christ's death for sin brings about a new life for those following him.[16]

Just as we shared in the guilt and condemnation of our first representative Adam, so now we share in the righteousness and life of our second and final representative Christ.

1 Corinthians 1:30: Christ Became Righteousness for Us

In 1 Corinthians 1:30, Paul also speaks of our union with Christ: "And because of him [God] you are in Christ Jesus, who became to us wisdom from God, righteousness and sanctification and redemption." The first thing that needs to be cleared away is the idea that if the imputation of righteousness is implied here, then that must also mean we are imputed with wisdom,

16. Vickers, *Jesus' Blood and Righteousness*, 184–85.

sanctification, and redemption.[17] First, wisdom in this context refers exactly to what Paul says it refers to, namely, the wisdom of God displayed in the gospel of Christ crucified, which in the eyes of the world is foolishness. The radical otherworldly act of God in the cross of Christ is the wisdom that turns the wisdom of the world on its head. Christ displayed the wisdom of God on the cross for us. There is no reason to say that if righteousness is imputed here, then wisdom must be too.

The same thing is true of sanctification and redemption. Paul speaks of three aspects of the salvation we have in Christ who, in his death on the cross, is the manifestation of the wisdom of God. The wisdom of God here is Christ and his cross, and from this wisdom flow three things that we have in our status before God. The concept of sanctification is sometimes spoken of only in terms of the ongoing work of God in the life of the believer, and certainly it is that, but that is not all there is to it, and it is not what Paul has in mind here.

The word *sanctification* (*hagiosmos*) is part of a word group from which we also get *holy*, *holiness*, and *saint(s)*. These words are usually connected to a status already held before God, as they are at the beginning of 1 Corinthians 1. Paul addresses the Corinthians as those "sanctified" in Christ who are called "saints." The sanctification that the Corinthians have in Christ is not just the ongoing work of God in their lives; it is also a status they already possess through Christ. They are called "holy ones" or "saints" because of what God has done for them in Christ. Later, Paul speaks of sanctification, along with justification, as something already given to the Corinthians in Christ: "But you were washed, you were sanctified, you were justified in the name of the Lord Jesus Christ, and by the Spirit of God" (1 Cor. 6:11). Without a doubt, the New Testament writers speak frequently of

---

17. N. T. Wright argues for this—that imputation cannot be in view here in regard to righteousness because that would mean, incorrectly, that the other elements are imputed as well—in *What St. Paul Really Said: Was Paul of Tarsus the Real Founder of Christianity?* (Grand Rapids: Eerdmans, 1997), 123. He continues to argue, in a similar way, against imputation in this text on the same grounds, in *Justification: God's Plan & Paul's Vision*, 155–58.

the ongoing work that God does in the lives of believers through the Spirit, which we call sanctification, but we have to be careful that we do not read theological concepts—even correct ones—back into words. This status, moreover, is not ours through the imputation of Christ's sanctification but is ours through the work of Christ on the cross and is applied by the Spirit.

Similarly, redemption refers not to something imputed to us but to God's saving act in Christ in which believers are redeemed (bought or purchased) through the cross. Paul speaks of redemption as something we have in Christ in Colossians 1:14, and as what we have "through his blood" in Ephesians 1:7. Christ became our redemption by dying for our sins under God's judgment, and his blood paid the penalty that our sins deserved. Again, there is no reason to assert that redemption is imputed to us.

That wisdom, sanctification, and redemption are not imputed is beyond question. Righteousness, however, is imputed to us—that is how it becomes ours in Christ. The Bible teaches this from Genesis 15:6 onward. First Corinthians 1:30 does not speak of *how* we acquire this righteous status, only that it is ours in Christ; the "how" question is answered largely from reading other texts. Paul does say that what we have in Christ comes "to us . . . from God," but how that applies to us in terms of righteousness cannot be drawn out of this text by itself—but then, there is no reason why it has to be. The important issue in this text is not imputation but that the righteousness we have before God comes as his gift to us in Christ.

Conclusion

When Isaiah says, famously, that "all our righteous acts are like filthy rags" (64:6),[18] he confesses the sinfulness of the nation that led to the exile, the devastation of Jerusalem, and the destruction of the temple. The nation, because of its idolatry and injustice, suffers under the curses outlined in Deuteronomy. Isaiah 63:7–19

18. NIV.

recounts God's grace toward them, particularly in the exodus. God has a perfect record of faithfulness to his people. They, on the other hand, have been everything but faithful. Nevertheless, God is their Father (v. 16), and Isaiah looks forward to a day when God will create descendants from Jacob and Judah (65:9), and ultimately a new heaven and a new earth in which all past sins are forgotten forever (v. 17). There all the nations will gather and worship the Lord. Isaiah strikes an ominous note as well—God will come furiously in judgment (66:15–16). God will both judge and save. The message of Isaiah 63–66 is about the pure grace of God in salvation, his rightful wrath and punishment of sin, and his unswerving devotion to his promise to Abraham. As for the people, they are debtors to his mercy alone. Their track record is one of idol worship, rebellion, and oppression. They, like all people, have nothing to bring to God but their sin. It is a study in the contrast between God's righteousness and our righteousness.

When we say with Isaiah that all our own righteousness is as clean as filthy rags, we own our sin and confess our total reliance on God's grace and mercy. God answers by pouring out his righteous judgment on his perfectly obedient son, Jesus Christ, exchanging our sin for his righteousness, and in doing so extends salvation to us through faith in him. That is the power of God unto salvation, witnessed by the Law and the Prophets and revealed in Christ, in whom we are made righteous, justified by God.

7

Faith Works: The Life of the Justified

RIPE, RED APPLES on a tree do not exist by themselves. They are dependent, wholly dependent, on healthy roots—the part of the tree that we do not see but without which there is no fruit. The relationship between root and fruit is a time-tested picture of the relationship between faith and the works that grow from it. This chapter is about that relationship.

- Justification and Faith in James
- Paul on Romans 2:13
- Holding to James and Paul

"Justified by faith alone." How familiar we are with that phrase. It is one of the famous "alones" (or *solas*) of the Reformation—grace alone; faith alone; Christ alone; Scripture alone; God's glory alone. The idea of faith alone is implied throughout the Bible, but the phrase itself appears in only one place, James 2:24: "You see that a person is justified by works and not by faith alone." According to James, it may seem that at least one of the tenets of the Reformation, not to mention Paul, is completely wrong. On the other hand, maybe James got it wrong, or maybe James and Paul simply disagree. Differences like this one have caused all sorts of problems down through the centuries.

It is safe to say that everyone has felt tension when reading, say, James 2:14–26 and Romans 3:21–31 together. Who has not, at some point, thought something like this: "How can I make them agree?" Some take the approach that our business is not to worry about agreement but to let each add his distinctive voice to Scripture, and then live with the tension. I am sympathetic with that sentiment, and I am all for living with certain tensions and certainly for allowing every part of Scripture to speak for itself. On the other hand, we should want to know how the Bible fits together, particularly given what evangelicals confess to believe about who God is and how he inspired the Bible, and when the discussion centers on something as vital as justification.

We might conclude that James does not really mean what he seems to be saying. Some suggest that James and Paul mean different things by "justification." Perhaps James is dealing with a deficient form of Paul's theology that takes justification by faith to mean simple agreement with facts and then downplays obedience as a result. There is also the practical approach of ignoring James altogether and preaching virtually everything else in the Bible except Revelation and the Song of Solomon. I am not content with any of those solutions, particularly the last one, and while I do not think that my purpose in life is to make James and Paul agree with one another, I do believe that they agree. The trick is to remember that James (writing before Paul) and Paul wrote to different contexts that faced different struggles and opposition. Here is what I believe about James: (1) He means what he says; (2) "justified" does not mean something radically different to James than it does to Paul, though different emphases may be placed on it at different times; and, (3) while it is possible that James is dealing with a bad form of Pauline theology that Paul himself would reject, such a reconstruction is not necessary for understanding what James has to say. James is out to condemn justification by *demon faith*—the kind of faith that shows itself in words alone, even ultrareligious words.

Justification and Faith in James

Setting the Context

By the time James 2 begins, it is already clear that for James everything good, including salvation, comes from God. Whoever experiences trials—which, James implies, serve a divine purpose to refine faith (1:3)—should pray and believe that God will grant the wisdom needed to persevere and will faithfully act to answer such a prayer (v. 5). The God-given reward for this divinely empowered perseverance is life (v. 12). He then makes this declaration, vital for understanding in the following chapter on faith and works.

> Every good gift and every perfect gift is from above, coming down from the Father of lights with whom there is no variation or shadow due to change. Of his own will he brought us forth by the word of truth, that we should be a kind of firstfruits of his creatures. (vv. 17–18)

There is no question that James understands salvation (and I am using that term in the broadest sense) as solely the work of God from conversion (God "brought us forth") to perseverance, all the way to final, eschatological life, "which God has promised to those who love him" (v. 12). James would no doubt affirm "soli Deo gloria"—"to God alone be the glory."

Not Just Hearers but Doers. James is out to overturn all religion that exists in name and word only. Following the teaching of Jesus, James says, "be doers of the word, and not hearers only, deceiving yourselves" (v. 22; cf. Matt. 7:24, 26; Luke 6:47, 49). He warns against the self-deception of presuming a relationship with God on the basis of words alone. He likens such a person to someone who glances into a mirror and then turns away and forgets what he looks like (1:23–24). He then gives a concrete example: the person who thinks that he is a follower of God but who cannot control what comes out of his mouth—"This person's religion is worthless" (v. 26). On the other hand, true believers will seek out justice and the well-being of the helpless (e.g., widows and orphans), and they will make it their business to live a life in contrast with the world (v. 27). Such ideas abound in James, and while it is often, and rightly, noted that James has a special emphasis on the poor, disenfranchised, and needy, he is not driven merely by social conscience. James shows what the true Christian life should look like, what should concern Christians, how they should be characterized, and what actions and behaviors are incompatible with true faith in God, calling one's confession into question.

The center point in James's treatment of these themes is 2:8: "You shall love your neighbor as yourself," which James refers to as "the royal law according to the Scripture." Like Paul (Gal. 5:14), James reduces the great commandments down to one. Also like Paul, the first part, "Love the Lord your God," is assumed, and James concerns himself with how love for God is displayed.[1] Of course this is nothing new, because love for neighbor was *always* an expression of love for God, just as love for God is meant to flow out into love for neighbor. Leviticus 19:18, from which James draws his quote, is surrounded by commands, most of which are moral, social, and ethical, punctuated with the phrases: "You shall be holy, for I the LORD your God am holy," "I am the LORD your God," and "I am the LORD." Knowledge of God and love for God are the foundations for obedience to the command to love one's neighbor. This is instructive for chapter 2, where James emphasizes works as the display of true faith in God.

Judges with Evil Thoughts and Transgressors. Partiality is a sin to which we pay very little attention. In many circles it is common practice, and any implications of sinfulness are virtually ignored. Yet we do it all the time when we elevate personalities to rock star status in the church and foster personality cults, all the while ignoring the needs of the people we see every week.

1. Bauckham has a very good discussion of James's quote of Leviticus 19 (the text from which "you shall love your neighbor as yourself" is taken), and also how the role of the *Shema* (Deut. 6:4–5; more on that text below) makes it certain that the first command, "love the Lord your God," is taken for granted. Richard Bauckham, *James* (Milton Park, NY: Rutledge, 1999), 142–47.

If, for instance, a famous pastor or speaker visited your church this week, you would be eager to speak to him, spend time with him, and perhaps take him out for lunch after church—none of which is wrong in and of itself. It would be strange, to say the least, for a guest speaker to arrive and have to get his own taxi from the airport, find a hotel room, make his way to the church, and be ignored during his visit. But what if, on the same day that the famous pastor is in town, a family visits from off the street? Would they get the same kind of reception? In most places they probably would not be asked to move to the back of the church, but would they be made to feel equally as welcome? I am sure that in many churches they would be, but ask it on a personal level—if your favorite preacher/theologian came to your church this weekend and a homeless family came in the door at the same moment, where would your attention go?

Take one more scenario: Say that a rich man is interested in joining your church just when you need money for the building fund, to pay off debt, or to expand your church's ministry and support of missions—he could be the answer to all those prayers. At the same time, a man with a very low income wants to join—someone who is not in the position to contribute financially to the ministry. Would both men receive the same treatment? Would both be on track to become an insider among the leaders? Would visions for future ministry and expansion be shared equally with both men? This is something akin to the challenges faced among those to whom James writes, and he accuses those who show partiality of being "judges with evil thoughts" (2:4) and "transgressors" (v. 9). These are the sorts of people who confess one thing but whose actions call their confession into question.

Members of the New Covenant. James begins chapter 2 by addressing his audience as believers: "My brothers, show no partiality as you hold the faith in our Lord Jesus Christ, the Lord of glory" (v. 1). Their faith in Jesus should be the motivating factor, the fuel, for obedience to the command to show no partiality. James expects that if they truly are believers, then they will do what he says. He then offers a scene taken no doubt from actual life, similar to the ones above. A rich person enters the congregation and receives special attention, while a poor person comes in and gets second-class treatment.[2] James has no patience for such behavior and does not try to water down the seriousness of such actions. To make matters worse, the very people to whom they pander are the same people who harm them (v. 6). The sin of partiality is no better than the sins of adultery and murder— God condemns them all (vv. 10–11). Again in harmony with the teaching of Jesus (Matt. 5:19), he reminds them that breaking one commandment means breaking the entire law, and similar to Paul (Gal. 3:10), he warns of punishment (James 2:10). James's message is not, however, that his readers had better keep the Mosaic law; it is that they are living in a new era, alluded to when he admonishes them: "So speak and so act as those who are to be judged under the law of liberty" (v. 12). This is not the easiest phrase to interpret, but along with his expectation that they can fulfill the second great command (v. 8), James points them to the reality of the new covenant, of which they are members.[3]

The phrase "law of liberty" is found only in James (1:25; 2:12), and he does not explain exactly what he means by it. I take it to refer to the freedom to fulfill the ethical and moral precepts of the law—the very things that James emphasizes throughout his letter. Bauckham is right to connect it to 1:18 ("brought us forth by the word of truth," i.e., the gospel) and to the Old Testament background of Ezekiel 11 and 36, where God promises new hearts and his Spirit, through which his people will "walk in my statutes and keep my rules and obey them" (Ezek. 11:19–20; cf. 36:26–28).[4] James assumes a situation in which God has put his law in their hearts in fulfillment of his new covenant promise (Jer. 31:33).[5] If this background is in view, and there are good indications that

2. This scene reflects the social justice commands found in Lev. 19 (vv. 9–11; 13–17; divided only by a command to honor the Lord's name in verse 12) that lead up to the love command in v. 18.

3. See Christopher W. Morgan, *A Theology of James* (Phillipsburg, NJ: P&R Publishing, 2010), 121.

4. Bauckham, *James*, 146.

5. Ibid.

it is, then James is telling his readers that they must behave as those who have their hearts prepared to hear, accept, and put his teaching into practice. That is the same expectation shared by the New Testament writers generally—their teaching, like all Scripture, is meant as a means of teaching, reproof, correction, and "training in righteousness" (2 Tim. 3:16). They are free not only to hear commands but to obey them from the heart. Otherwise their faith and confession are false, and they are under condemnation.

Faith That Works

The big idea in James 2 is the nature of true faith and its evidence. James does not speak of faith as a series of steps, or paint a picture of "carnal Christians" over against mature Christians—no first-, second-, or third-chair Christians here. Nevertheless, James is writing to people who have failed to live up to their confession of faith, and his purpose in writing is to correct that failure. He does not assume that the partiality, backbiting, and other sins that he mentions mean that his readers are therefore necessarily unbelievers, but that their behavior calls their faith into question. There is only one kind of faith in Christ—the type that flows out into obedience. James asks, "What good is it, my brothers, if someone says he has faith but does not have works? Can that faith save him?" (v. 14).

The key word in verse 14 is *that*, as in "that faith." In Greek there is no pronoun, only the article.[6] This is why the RSV translates it "Can faith save you?" But the ESV and NASB are surely correct to translate the phrase "that faith." The NIV rendering of "such faith" fits the context as well. These translations insert *that* or *such* to point back to the kind of faith that James speaks of in the verse—the so-called faith that someone claims to have but which is shown to be false because it does not have works. It does not make sense for James to identify a particular kind of

6. The definite article (*the*) is used in Greek far more than in English in general, and it is very common for it to appear with nouns such as *faith*. Much of the time, the Greek article is not translated into English due to the difference between how the article is used in Greek and in English. In this verse there is no call for including *the* in the translation.

faith and then go on to ask if faith in general can save. It is false faith, not faith, that is on trial. James asks whether empty faith can save, not whether faith can save.[7] The addition of the English word *that* is faithful to James's intent. If James were writing in English today, he might place quotation marks around the word *faith* and italicize *that*: "Can *that* 'faith' save him?"

As usual, James gives a specific illustration to apply what he is teaching: "If a brother or sister is poorly clothed and lacking in daily food, and one of you says to them, 'Go in peace, be warmed and filled,' without giving them the things needed for the body, what good is that?" (vv. 15–16). James's point is that words cannot feed a person or put clothes on his back. Regardless of how pious the blessing may sound, it is really a curse, or at the very least a lie. After all, if the person who recites the blessing really cared about his brother or sister's well-being, if he truly wanted him to be blessed, then he would give him clothes and something to eat. The phrase "what good is that?" is basically parallel to "can that faith save him?" What good is an empty blessing on an empty stomach? What good is it to say you have faith when there is no fruit in your life to show it? This is the conclusion James draws: "So also faith by itself, if it does not have works, is dead" (v. 17).

Showing Faith versus Saying Faith. In 2:18–23, James shows what he means by saying that faith without works is dead. Like any good teacher, James anticipates the sorts of questions that will arise from his teaching—and he knows the people to whom he writes. The "you" in these verses is probably not his readers but a would-be conversation partner who raises the kind of questions that James expects his readers to have.[8]

The point that James makes in these verses is that faith does not consist in a confession alone. Faith cannot be in word only; it should show itself in actions as well. Before going even one step further, we need to acknowledge that James does not entertain questions about how works may be false, nor does he point out

---

7. As Morgan puts it, "James considers this opposing view of faith to be bogus." Morgan, *A Theology of James*, 134.

8. Bauckham, *James*, 58.

that works may be motivated by something other than faith, nor does he stop to warn against works righteousness—those are questions generated by debates and discussions that James is not having. They are good questions and important points to make, but James is not concerned here with what he is not saying or the extremes to which what he says may be taken. Our first priority is to let James speak without our feeling a need to help him articulate better than he does. Of course works can be false, and of course works righteousness is a deadly problem, but in this text the works to which James refers are those done out of true faith. The idea in verse 18 is that you cannot see faith apart from works. We need to keep the discussion there for the time being.

Demon Faith. The words "you believe God is one" in verse 19 allude to the *Shema*, the revered confession of Deuteronomy 6:4–5: "Hear, O Israel: The LORD our God, the LORD is one. You shall love the LORD your God with all your heart and with all your soul and with all your might." Reciting the *Shema* is a confession of orthodoxy, a confession that acknowledges who God is, what he is like, and what is expected of those who follow him. No one could claim to be a follower of God and deny the *Shema*. The positive response "you do well" is not meant as a compliment. It is similar to the way we say "good catch" when the ball goes right through someone's hands. What follows it supports taking it this way: "Even the demons believe—and shudder." In other words, if you are banking on your orthodox confession alone, if you are reciting a creed, however venerable, and if you think that such a confession or creed by itself proves something, then you have risen to the level of demons—congratulations.

It is not difficult to find examples in the New Testament of the kind of faith that demons possess. The first example that comes to mind is the encounter that Jesus has with the demoniac in the region of the Gerasenes. The demon who possesses a man pleads with Jesus not to bother him: "What have you to do with me, Jesus, Son of the Most High God? I adjure you by God, do not torment me!" (Mark 5:7). The demon (or demons, since he calls himself "Legion") knows exactly who Jesus is and what he is capable of doing. Luke includes that the demons plead for Jesus not to throw them into "the abyss," which tells us that even they are terrified of the place they call home (cf. Rev. 9:1; 20:1). Although they face such dire circumstances, their "faith" could rise no higher than mere recognition of Jesus as the Son of God, and terror. So the demons "believe" in Jesus; that is, they believe who he is, but clearly they do not place their trust in him as Lord (whether they could do so is beside the point). So the demons can recite something like the *Shema*, and probably know the depths of its implications more than we do, but their knowledge of orthodoxy is of no use. Moreover, as opposed to those who merely "believe that God is one," at least that knowledge causes demons to cringe in fear. This passage ought to cause us to reflect on our own tendency to trust in our own brand of confession as though it were enough to make us true believers in Jesus Christ. No amount of orthodox knowledge is of any benefit unless that knowledge shows itself in speaking, acting, and living out the faith we claim to confess.

The Argument from Scripture: Abraham

If a reader, familiar only with the writings of Paul, had to guess what text James might use to support his teaching, he would probably not pick Genesis 15:6: Abraham "believed the LORD, and he counted it to him as righteousness." After all, that is Paul's go-to text to support justification by faith apart from works. But that is exactly the text James chooses. He is adamant about it, too: "Do you want to be shown, you foolish person, that faith apart from works is useless?" (2:20). He then answers the question with a short story of Abraham as though to say, "How could it be any clearer?" We should note, though, that before quoting Genesis 15, James goes to the story of Abraham and Isaac at Moriah (Genesis 22) and asks, "Was not Abraham our father justified by works when he offered up his son Isaac on the altar?" (James 2:21). Seeing the gap between the Abraham/Isaac story and the quote from years earlier in Abraham's life is the key for understanding what James has to say.

Justified by Faith or by Works: Hebron or Moriah? Paul and James use the same word (*edikaiōthē*), which translates as "justified" (Rom. 4:2; James 2:21). The word can mean "vindicate" or "show to be in the right," and can also refer to being declared and/or counted righteous, receiving God's gift of righteousness. Sometimes the line between the uses of the word is blurry, and we should beware of trying to separate the senses of the word as though they carry radically different meanings. This is not to say that the word, or any word, has multiple meanings every time it appears, but simply to recognize that declaring to be righteous and vindicating a declaration of righteousness (both appear in James and Paul) are not at opposite ends of the spectrum.

Paul says, "If Abraham was justified by works, he has something to boast about, but not before God" (Rom. 4:2), and James says it is clear that Abraham was justified by his works. They both quote Genesis 15:6, but we should remember that Paul quotes it twice in Romans 4 (vv. 3, 22), and the second quote follows his comments on Abraham's perseverance—we will return to that second citation in Romans 4 shortly. The thing to keep in mind is that James and Paul (at least in Rom. 4:1–8) are out to show two different things. Paul proves that his teaching of justification by faith apart from works is not novel but is the way people have always been made right with God. James is out to show that saving faith is evidenced in its actions. One focuses on the faith as the root, while the other focuses on works as the necessary fruit of faith. James, as it were, stands on Mount Moriah with Abraham and Isaac, looks back to Hebron (Abraham's location in Genesis 15) and the great declaration made in Genesis 15:6, and says, "See, that was no empty proclamation, nor was Abraham's faith simply an agreement with facts; and if you want proof, just look at what happened with Isaac." James's assessment is not really that different from what the angel of the Lord said to Abraham, "for now I know you fear God, seeing you have not withheld your son, your only son, from me" (Gen. 22:12). Abraham's actions on Moriah gave evidence of his justifying faith.

The larger context of Genesis 22 supports this conclusion, and also takes us back to ideas discussed in detail earlier in this book. Abraham's actions are met with a blessing, or rather a repeat blessing, for the angel repeats promises familiar in the Abraham story.

> And the angel of the LORD called to Abraham a second time from heaven and said, "By myself I have sworn, declares the LORD, because you have done this and have not withheld your son, your only son, I will surely bless you, and I will surely multiply your offspring as the stars of heaven and as the sand that is on the seashore. And your offspring shall possess the gate of his enemies, and in your offspring shall all the nations of the earth be blessed, because you have obeyed my voice." (Gen. 22:15–18)

Genesis 12, 15, and 17 should be ringing in the ears of anyone reading these verses. Had God not already promised all these things, and was not the covenant sealed in Genesis 15? Were these blessings and promises, moreover, made on the basis of Abraham's faith in God? Clearly the answer is "yes" to both questions. God's promises are sealed in an oath, and he will keep his word, but God plans on keeping his word with a particular kind of people—those who follow him in obedience. The promises will be kept unconditionally, and their fulfillment is not contingent on obedience; the fulfillment of the promises is concurrent, or parallel, with obedience. This does not make faith and works identical, but it shows the inseparability of the two. God's people, who are his through faith and who have received new hearts through the Spirit, will act like God's people, and what he says about them will be shown to be true. Both God and his justified people will be vindicated.

Paul, on the other hand, begins in Hebron, the point at which Scripture tells of God's declaration that Abraham was counted righteous by faith apart from works (Rom. 4:3). As Romans 4 further unfolds, Paul again quotes Genesis 15:6 after asserting that Abraham continued to believe in the promise to the nations and "did not weaken in faith" in the face of old age and Sarah's infertility, nor "waver concerning the promise of God, but he grew strong in his faith" because he knew "that God was able to do what he had promised" (Rom. 4:18–21). Then Paul says "that [what he has just said in vv. 18–21] is why his faith was 'counted to him as righteousness'" (v. 22). He is not saying that his faith was counted as righteousness *because* he would end up persevering, but that his perseverance proved that what was declared in Hebron was exactly right—God's counting of Abraham's faith as righteousness was shown to be true. So in the verses leading up to and including the second quote of Genesis 15 in Romans 4, we see that Paul is not saying something radically different from James; we could even say that they agree.

Fulfilling Scripture. Paul's "that is why" is quite similar to James's statement that Abraham's works "fulfilled" Genesis 15:6 (James 2:23). The word *fulfilled* does not mean that Abraham's works made the Scripture true—Scripture that could have been false if Abraham had gone a different way—but that Abraham's works brought the declaration in Hebron to its appointed end. The declaration was meant to be displayed so that God's word would be vindicated. God declared Abraham's faith as righteousness, and Abraham's actions, particularly his test with Isaac, affirmed the truth of Scripture. Similarly, James says one verse earlier that Abraham's faith was brought to completion by his works (v. 22). Abraham's faith was not lacking—his faith had justified him in the sight of God—but if it were true faith, then works must flow from it, "if faith is understood as wholehearted commitment to God and God's will."[9] When James says that "faith was active along with his works," there is no sense of a double basis for justification, that of both faith and works. But faith, the single foundation for justification, works—Abraham was justified by faith alone, but his justifying faith was not alone.

9. Bauckham, *James*, 121.

This way of understanding James helps make sense of verse 24, which if taken by itself seems to overthrow not only Paul but Moses as well. James has already shown that in his discussion, "faith alone" means no faith at all. In the same way, "works" in James 2 refers to the works that flow from true faith, the works that show faith to be true, justifying faith. Verse 24 can be paraphrased like this: "We see that a person is justified when we see the works that flow from true faith and not by demon faith alone." His second illustration, Rahab (a striking contrast with Abraham in a Jewish setting!), proves the same point. There is nothing in Scripture about the declaration of Rahab's faith as righteousness, but we know she was counted righteous because we can see evidence of her faith when she helped the two Israelite spies escape from Jericho (v. 25; cf. Joshua 2). The writer to the Hebrews, who defines faith as "the assurance of things hoped for, the conviction of things not seen" (11:1), commends Rahab for her faith, and the reason he gives for the commendation is "because she had given a friendly welcome to the spies" (v. 31). He would agree that her faith was active along with her works. The final verse in James 2 caps off the discussion with a definite word that seals the meaning of the entire chapter: "faith apart from works is dead," a statement Paul would no doubt affirm.

Speaking of Paul, at this point it is fitting to consider one of the most difficult texts in his letters in regard to justification, one that causes about as much trouble to Bible readers as James 2 because, like James, he seems to be saying that works are the basis of justification.

Paul on Romans 2:13

"For it is not the hearers of the law who are righteous before God, but the doers of the law who will be justified" (Rom. 2:13). Without doubt, this text causes as much anxiety as any text in Paul's letters. Those who do the law will be justified. How can that idea possibly fit with what Paul says in so many other places?

Just one chapter later in Romans we read that "by works of the law no human being will be justified in his sight" (3:20). Writing years earlier to the churches in Galatia, Paul says, "by works of the law no one will be justified" (Gal. 2:16). Soon after that, quoting Habakkuk, he says, "Now it is evident that no one is justified before God by the law, for 'The righteous shall live by faith'" (3:11). These verses appear to stand in opposition to Romans 2:13.

The Negative Role of the Law

In addition to explicit statements that seem to contradict Romans 2:13, there is also Paul's general attitude toward the law—in terms of its inability to make people right with God—that makes this verse seem more confusing. Before unpacking Romans 2:13, it is a good idea to reconsider Paul's negative discussion of the law. By negative I mean that it serves to reveal sinfulness and serves as a standard of judgment against sin. Here are a few examples.

- "Through the law comes knowledge of sin" (Rom. 3:20).
- "The law brings wrath" (4:15).
- "The law came in to increase the trespass" (5:20).
- "The very commandment that promised life proved to be death to me" (7:10).

When reading texts like these, it is essential to remember that Paul is not speaking of the law as negative, or much less evil, in itself. To the contrary, "the law is holy, and the commandment ["do not covet"] is holy and righteous and good" (7:12). Paul, I am sure, agreed with every word of Psalm 119. But the holiness of the law does not mean it has the wherewithal to grant life.[10] Paul is speaking about what the law does and the effects it has

10. See the discussion of Paul's negative statements about the law in connection with Pss. 19 and 119 in Thomas R. Schreiner, *40 Questions about Christians and Biblical Law* (Grand Rapids: Kregel, 2010), 85–87.

on people. The problem is not with the law but with sin, and the law is not able to deal ultimately with sin. What the law does in effect is similar to shining a spotlight onto a dark stage. It focuses all attention on what is there. A spotlight shining on a performer on the stage does not create the performer, but it shows his presence on the stage. The law does not create sin from nothing, but it provides a clear revelation of God's will and righteous standards by which sin is judged. It shows how short people fall in doing and attaining the righteousness that is acceptable and pleasing to God, and it provides a public, objective basis for condemnation of the world.

The law is powerless to hinder sin and ends up only making sin all the more heinous because once the law comes, no one can say, "I didn't know." It is wicked to steal, and everyone knows it innately because what God desires of us is ingrained on our hearts (Rom. 2:14–15), but it is even more wicked to steal when you have a law that tells you it is wrong and what will happen if you do it. Given the statements about the impossibility of justification on the basis of the Sinai covenant and the covenant law, and Paul's negative assessment of the law's ability to curb sin, we are in a better position to read Romans 2:13.

Doing the Law and Being Justified in the Future

First there is the matter of the context of Romans 2:13. Paul is establishing for the sake of the Jews that they, like the Gentiles, are without excuse for their sin. Each person will stand before God on the basis of his or her own life. The main idea in 2:1–11 is that God shows no favoritism but judges each person accordingly. There will be eternal life for those "who by patience in well-doing seek for glory and honor and immortality" (v. 7). On the other hand, for "those who are self-seeking and do not obey the truth, but obey unrighteousness, there will be wrath and fury" (v. 8). With or without the law, all sinners will be punished (v. 12). The scene of this text is set in the future. Paul speaks of the final, eschatological judgment day. This future orientation continues in verse 13. On the final day, those who have done the law will be justified.

Hypothetically Justified?

For many, including myself at various points in the past, the way to understand this text is to take what Paul is saying as hypothetical. Yes, the doers of the law will be justified, *but* we know that no one can keep the law fully, so while it is true that *if* someone keeps the law he will be justified, the fact of the matter is that no one can keep it. So in reality no one will be justified by doing the law. Therefore, Paul is speaking hypothetically. The Achilles' heel of this interpretation, however, is found just a little way forward in the chapter when Paul makes a distinction between the letter of the law and the Spirit (vv. 25–29). Paul denies that merely having the law and having the outward sign of it, circumcision, are grounds for salvation. A Jew can be circumcised, but if he breaks the law, he becomes like a Gentile (v. 26). If a Gentile keeps the moral principles of the law (v. 14), then even though uncircumcised, he becomes like a Jew and will stand as a witness against Jews who, although circumcised, failed to keep the law. The result of all this is that Paul is making the distinction—via Deuteronomy—between physical circumcision and circumcision of the heart, which, just as Jeremiah and Ezekiel foretold, means having the Spirit. Here is how Paul wraps up the whole discussion:

> For no one is a Jew who is merely one outwardly, nor is circumcision outward and physical. But a Jew is one inwardly, and circumcision is a matter of the heart, by the Spirit, not by the letter. His praise is not from man but from God. (vv. 28–29)

For at least three reasons, Paul is *not* speaking hypothetically here. First, his "if . . . then" statements in verses 25–26 are not hypothetical. It would be extraordinarily odd for Paul to say, "Hypothetically speaking, if you break the law, your circumcision will not be of any use to you." That would be the same as saying

157

that in reality, breaking the law does not ultimately matter all that much as long as you are circumcised (a sort of physical assent to the truth). That is the exact opposite of the point Paul makes every time he mentions circumcision in his letters. Second, Paul is saying that the future has come, the new covenant is established, and now all the people of God obey from a heart filled with the Spirit. Third, in verse 29, the "praise" from God, given the future context of the passage and the clearly eschatological context of the word in other places (1 Cor. 4:5; 1 Peter 1:7), refers to the final reward of eternal life. Those who obey through the Spirit will be rewarded with eternal life by God on the last day. As in Romans 2:13, Paul draws a direct line between life in the present and judgment in the future. What happens in the present does not stay in the present.

Fulfilling the Promise

If Romans 2:13 is not hypothetical—and 2:25–29 makes it unlikely—then are there two, or even more, justifications? After all, Paul can speak of being justified as a present reality (Rom. 5:1; 8:30; 1 Cor. 6:11), but here he speaks of justification as a future event, and this is not the only time that justification is linked to the future (e.g., Rom. 5:18, 21). There are not multiple justifications, nor several temporary verdicts handed down from God. If Paul were asked, "Are you justified?," his answer would not be, "For now, at least." It may sound a little confusing, but God's declaration of righteousness over the believer in Christ is his future, end-time verdict given in the present. To put it another way, when we come to faith in Christ, our justification in the present is *the same justification that will be declared publicly in the future at the resurrection and judgment*. In the future, those in Christ will hear the verdict "righteous" passed upon them, and these people will be those who were doers of the law through the Spirit. For Paul, like the rest of Scripture, there is no conception that obedience to God is a totally separate issue from salvation.

The Fruit, Not the Root

Red flags may be rising after that last part. Before the flags hit full staff, pause and remember Genesis 18:17–19 and Joshua 24:14—one cannot be a true child of Abraham and go back to Ur to worship idols. The promise that *will be fulfilled* will come true to and through those who do "righteousness and justice" (Gen. 18:19). Obedience, doing righteousness and justice, doing the law, is not the *basis* of justification in Romans 2:13. The basis of justification is the cross and resurrection of Christ. Prior obedience was not the reason God made his covenant with Abraham and promised to make him a great nation and bless the world through him and his seed. Obedience from the heart is the divinely ordained, and therefore necessary, action that provides evidence of inheritance of God's promises. The cross and its vindication at the resurrection seal the new covenant, and from these events flows the fulfillment of the promise of a circumcised heart, the gift of the Holy Spirit.

Justification is declared over those who trust in Christ, period. Those who trust in Christ receive new hearts through the Spirit and do justice and righteousness—the essence of obedience found in the law. That is what characterizes a member of the new covenant. Ultimately, we could say that those who love God and love their neighbor are those who will be justified. So, on the last day, the final verdict of "righteous" will be declared publicly upon exactly the kind of people God said would inherit the promise—the same declaration now had by faith. The ground of that declaration will be faith in Christ (the root), and the evidence to vindicate God's declaration as true (as with Abraham, cf. Rom. 4) will be the obedience (the fruit) that is in keeping with membership in the new covenant.

Romans 2:13, including its context, is a foreshadow of something Paul will say in chapter 8. Speaking there about the new life in the Spirit, Paul says that God sent Jesus to die for sins (since the law could not change sinful nature) in order to bring about new covenant obedience: "in order that the righteous requirement of the law might be fulfilled in us, who walk not according

159

to the flesh but according to the Spirit" (v. 4). I do not think it is likely that Paul is speaking here of the imputation of Christ's righteousness as the fulfillment, but rather of what Christ's work accomplishes in us—through the Spirit, believers fulfill the "righteous requirement" or "righteous thing" (*dikaioma tou nomou)* of the law. Moreover, his language of walking in accordance with the Spirit makes believers' obedience the more likely interpretation of this verse. As for the "righteous requirement," Paul does not spell it out, but I think that it is justifiable to infer that the great commandments (love God and love neighbor),[11] the heart of the law, are implied in the statement. It is not the law of Moses *per se* but the aim of it that believers fulfill through the Spirit. In that case, Romans 8:4 describes the "doers of the law" of Romans 2:13. A final word is in order. This does not mean that justification is based on works done through us by the Spirit, or that justification is grounded in faith in Christ and God's knowledge of the obedience that each believer will render in life, but that the Spirit-driven obedience is part and parcel of the life of the justified. A tree is known by its fruit.

Holding to James and Paul

I once asked two New Testament scholars familiar with the modern justification debates what they believed to be the worst danger facing the church.[12] One said, "Antinomianism [lawlessness]: people think that because they have the righteousness of Christ, they can basically get away with living however they want. Sure, they believe sin is bad and should be avoided, but there is always that safety net." The other answered, "Legalism: the church is filled with people who practically believe that they are saved

11. It could also be summed up with "doing justice and righteousness," clear descriptions of the neighbor side of the two commandments. Paul himself says that "the whole law is summed up in one word: 'You shall love your neighbor as yourself'" (Gal. 5:14). In both a Mosaic and new covenant context, loving neighbor assumes, and is driven by, love for God.

12. I asked the question at different times, and here I am paraphrasing their responses, but these were real conversations, and my recounting of them is accurate.

by what they do." I could not agree more with both of them. The church is filled with antinomians and legalists. Speaking personally, I can attest that I am often antinomian and legalistic simultaneously. We all are at different points, though usually we tend to one direction or another, often according to what we feel needs most to be guarded against in the church. It is an oversimplification to say that James fights lawlessness while Paul fights legalism. Reading them together makes it more than evident that their differences have been greatly exaggerated. Anyone who thinks that obedience is less important or necessary to Paul than to James has simply never read Paul closely enough. The same can be said of anyone who thinks that James is practically a second-string apostle. We desperately need them both, and only by preaching and teaching both do we have an opportunity to guard against the extremes of antinomianism and legalism.

Paul recognized the possible extremes of his teaching on justification and gives a preemptive strike in Romans 6:1: "What shall we say then? Are we to continue to sin so that grace may abound?" But the possibility that his teaching might turn into lawlessness did not for a second stop him from proclaiming the message of justification by faith alone apart from works. If we are never accused of being antinomian, then, as Martyn Lloyd-Jones pointed out, we are probably not preaching the gospel.

For many people reading this book, there is probably little need to emphasize that we must preach an unadulterated doctrine of justification by faith. But for most of us in some sort of Reformational tradition, a nudge to preach James 2 and Romans 2 with the same boldness is likely in order. Of course we do preach them both, but how often do we misapply them by focusing mostly on what each text does *not* say? It is absolutely vital that we explain what a text does not mean; not to do so is an act of pastoral negligence. At the same time, like James, we must be bold to tell people that no amount of confessional orthodoxy is enough to save anyone, and that being a dyed-in-the-wool believer of justification by faith is not the same thing as trusting in Christ for salvation. We cannot skirt the new covenant reality that the true people of God are meant to live as those who have the Spirit and love God and neighbor from the (new) heart. At the same time, we must walk the fine line of urging God-given, new covenant obedience flowing from faith without causing people to look to their obedience as their assurance and rest—only God rightly judges on that score. Our assurance, as our justification, is in Christ alone, by grace alone, through faith alone. We believe that, but often we seek to justify ourselves apart from, or more typically in addition to, Christ. In the next chapter, that tendency and other pastoral applications of justification will bring this study to a close. What better place to end than in that eminently pastoral letter, Galatians?

Freedom: Justification Applied

Formerly, when you did not know God, you were enslaved to those that by nature are not gods. But now that you have come to know God, or rather to be known by God, how can you turn back again to the weak and worthless elementary principles of the world, whose slaves you want to be once more? (Gal. 4:8–9)

For freedom Christ has set us free; stand firm therefore, and do not submit again to a yoke of slavery. (Gal. 5:1)

IN THIS CHAPTER we visit the following subjects:

- Seeking Our Own Justification
- Falling from Grace
- Freedom in the Gospel
- Radical Freedom

Seeking Our Own Justification

It is easy to forget that justification is not first a matter for debate, or an ecclesial litmus test, or much less about listening for shibboleths that prove one is on the "right side" (defined of course by each particular side). I have lost count of the number of conversations I have had that *began* with someone's asking me whether Dr. X follows "the New Perspective," whether Pastor Y believes in justification by works, or even, shockingly, whether Mr. Z is a heretic or even a believer. My typical response is to ask what is meant by "New Perspective" or "works," or what it means to trust Christ for salvation. Let me be clear: such questions are vitally important and, when appropriate, must be asked. It is beyond doubt that we need to understand the positions held by those with whom we disagree. We have a responsibility to know where other views fall theologically and to explain exactly why we believe that opposing positions are incorrect and often dangerous. All that, however, cannot be the whole of our engagement with the doctrine of justification.

Our first concern should be about how our own views on justification play out in everyday life. I speak to those of us on the so-called traditional side of the debates. The greatest practical danger facing us does not come from without but from within. The matter is not whether we simply know the right things—anyone can read and amass knowledge—but whether our practices, attitudes, desires, and ambitions reflect what we know to be true. Our actions can belie our statements. We must always, in every generation, beware of tendencies to create grounds for our justification beyond Christ.

For that reason, we will take some time to consider Paul's letter to the Galatians and their propensity to look to something beyond or in addition to Christ for their justification. In this way, Galatians will serve as a lens through which we see the application of justification to our lives.

When Peter Came to Antioch

The confrontation between Paul and Peter in Antioch, narrated by Paul in Galatians 2, gives us a biblical example of how one can understand justification but act in ways that call that knowledge into question. When Peter ate with Gentiles in Antioch (v. 12), he showed that he believed there was no ethnic or cultural basis for justification. Anyone who believed in Christ and received the Spirit was an equal brother or sister in the faith. Later, however, when "men from James" showed up, Peter moved to the popular crowd's table. Table fellowship with Gentiles, who were uncircumcised and did not follow food and purity laws and were therefore unclean, was taboo for a Jew. For these Jewish Christians, that sort of thing should have gone by the wayside because of faith in Christ. Paul says that Peter's fear of "the circumcision party" motivated his change of behavior. Whatever the exact cause of the fear—whether Peter was personally self-conscious of his own standing with Jewish believers or whether he was afraid that word of what was going on in Antioch would get back to Jerusalem and cause more problems for believers there—the important point is that he compromised his belief about what made a person right in God's eyes. To make matters worse, even Paul's friend and longtime teacher in Antioch, Barnabas, was "led astray by their hypocrisy" (v. 13). Paul will have nothing of it.

Are You Justified by Faith or Not? Paul's assessment is simple: "their conduct was not in step with the truth of the gospel" (v. 14). It is clear that Paul is dealing with believers; otherwise, conduct according to the gospel would be irrelevant in this circumstance. He asks Peter how he, a Jew, can sometimes live like a Gentile but then later by his actions imply that the Gentiles need to become Jews. Like Paul, Peter is a Jew by birth and not a "Gentile sinner," but Paul reminds him that "we know that a person is not justified by works of the law but through faith in Jesus Christ, so we also have believed in Christ Jesus, in order to be justified by faith in Christ and not by works of the law, because by works of the law no one will be justified" (v. 16).[1] He does not teach Peter anything new but reminds him of what he already knows and believes. It is faith in Christ, not the works demanded by the law, that justifies.

1. "Gentile sinners" denotes the status or position of those who live outside the Mosaic covenant. Paul and Peter were not born Gentile sinners, but the covenantal barriers between Jews and Gentiles are gone.

Not only are works of the law unable to justify, but the law's time is past. When Paul says later, "through the law I died to the law" (v. 19), he is talking about Christ's death under the curse of the law as his death (and all believers') in union with Christ. He will expand on this idea later by explaining that the goal of the law was met in Christ, who died under its curse in order to bring about the fulfillment of the promise to Abraham (3:13–14), and that the law's purpose of exposing sin and leading to Christ and the gospel was accomplished (vv. 22–24).

The problem for the circumcision party, the Galatians enticed by them, and Peter (at least temporarily) is that they all failed to understand three things. First, the law was never meant to justify. Second, God's intended purpose for it was accomplished. Third, the Messiah had come and the era of law was over. Believing Jews had been set free from the curse of the law but were now trying to reach back and hold to particular points of law as part of their relationship with God in Christ. Through the gospel, Gentile believers were released from their slavery to the sin of idolatry, but were now tempted to believe that they must add works from the law to their faith in Christ. In light of the gospel, all attempts to find identity and self-justification on the basis of works are all the more horrible.

Mistaking Signs for the Destination. Nearly everyone has visited a theme park of some kind. As a child, my parents took me to Florida nearly every year to visit relatives, and on several occasions we went to Disney World and Epcot. One of the hardest things for a child who is traveling to Disney World is that the billboards that advertise the park start miles and miles before you arrive. The closer you get to the park, the more signs there are. The more billboards passed, the more the question, "Are we there yet?" is asked. The billboards entice the visitor with all the wonderful attractions. Cinderella's castle, Spaceship Earth, and rides like the Pirates of the Caribbean fill the roadside vista. Then, finally, after a lifetime, you reach the main gates, and the top of the castle and Spaceship Earth come into view. Granted, there are still parking lots the size of small cities to cross, ticket lines measured in geological time, and a monorail to ride, but you are there. All the waiting and anxiety are over and forgotten (at least by the children) in an instant. The billboards did their job, but they are no longer needed or thought of. There was never a time after reaching the Magic Kingdom that I asked my parents, "Can we go back and look at those billboards?" I did not want to see the billboards nor wish that there were a few standing around the park. Their job was done. The desire to add aspects of the law, or anything else, to faith in Christ is like getting to Disney World and longing for the billboard advertisements.[2]

Now that Christ has come, all the signs like the law, which served its divine purpose, are fulfilled. Now there is freedom in Christ; we are justified by faith. To fall back on the law, Mosaic or otherwise, is to enslave ourselves to things that could never save or justify us. Worse still, it amounts to "deserting him who called you in the grace of Christ and turning to another gospel—not that there is another one" (Gal. 1:6–7).

"Jesus and . . ."

Earlier I referred to a phenomenon that I, and others, call "Jesus *and* . . . ." Whether or not readers have heard it put that way, everyone has experienced it and practiced it. It simply refers to adding something, whether consciously or not, to Christ as the basis for our justification. We do it in all sorts of ways. In Galatia and other stops along Paul's missionary journeys, there was pressure to practice circumcision in addition to faith in Christ. For Paul, adding to Christ for justification meant preaching another gospel, which is no gospel at all.

Clearing Away Misunderstandings. Before going further, some qualifications are needed to ensure that everyone is on the same page. At this point someone might wonder how Paul is able to speak against circumcision in Galatia but then approve

---

2. Granted, like all illustrations, this one falls apart if pushed to an extreme. Once, after sharing this illustration, I was asked whether I believe there is no longer need to read or apply the Old Testament. Rest assured that is not my intention. The billboard story simply illustrates the difference between signs and destinations.

of Timothy's circumcision. Paul was free to have Timothy circumcised (Acts 16:3)—and Timothy was free to receive it!—to remove an obstacle for the gospel, but that was not a case of adding circumcision to faith in Christ as a requirement for being right with God. It was a matter of becoming a Jew to win Jews, of becoming "all things to all people, that by all means I might save some" (1 Cor. 9:20–22). We may choose, for instance, to eat certain foods and/or abstain from certain drinks either for personal reasons or to avoid offending those around us. For instance, I would never dream of eating pork in Muslim contexts because it would create yet another obstacle in a context laden with obstacles—but we must never make what we eat, drink, or abstain from a point of identifying ourselves in Christ. Our identification is only as sinners justified by God's free gift of righteousness.

Subtle Self-Justification. It is unlikely that members of the circumcision party will visit our churches and entice people away from justification by faith alone. It is also unlikely that church members will be drawn into keeping Mosaic food and purity laws as a way of adding to faith in Christ. In many of our churches we probably do not face overt and explicit opposition to justification by faith alone as Paul found in Galatia. Our tendencies toward self-justification are more subtle, but our motivation, however unconscious, is similar to what Paul fought in Galatia—we think we need more than Jesus to be right with God. And though we might not pursue avenues so immediately deadly as requiring adherence to the law for justification, the effect over time can be the same. Subtle does not equal better or less dangerous.

Enslaved to the "Good." Almost anything can become a means of justifying ourselves. At the top of the list is the temptation to find satisfaction and identity in our ministries, churches, gifts, and abilities. Even ministry entities that have justification and other Reformational doctrines at their core can become a means of seeking to be justified in addition to Christ. It can become "Jesus *and* our ministry." One of the first steps down this slippery slope is when we constantly define ourselves over against those who are not like us theologically, practically, or culturally.[3] It is good to distinguish ourselves according to our confessions and to set forth carefully our particular distinctives, but when we start to say, "We thank you, God, that we are not like those people," we should take stock of ourselves.

The second step is when the pronouns *we* and *our* become the most commonly used words in our ecclesial, communal, and institutional vocabulary. Success and growth, not bad things in the right measure and perspective, can lead to blindness to the fact that we rely on, are more focused on, and rest in our ministries rather than on Christ alone. Like circumcision and other laws in Galatia, our ministries can become the visible signs we point to and lean on as evidence that we are right with God. In other words, we can replace faith with the sight of our ministries. On the other side of the coin, we may be resting in the fact that we are *not* like those who tout their gifts and ministries. There is a "humble" self-justification that is every bit as deadly as arrogance and self-importance. Everyone can pray the Pharisee's prayer. Self-justification is an equal opportunity destroyer and never discriminates.

"I Am of Paul; I Am of Apollos." There is also a tendency to seek justification through association. Attending a particular church, school, or conference can become a practical means of adding to faith in Christ if it becomes the chief way we perceive ourselves and our standing before God. Knowing (or just meeting) a well-known evangelical pastor or speaker can be a gratifying experience, but if those whom we know, meet, and listen to are the first figures who come to mind when we conceive of who we are as Christians, then we are in danger of seeking to justify ourselves apart from Christ. Likewise, sitting under the preaching of a pastor well known for his theological and expositional skills is a tremendous blessing, but if we come to

3. When I say "theologically," I do not only mean in comparison with people in radically different confessional (or nonconfessional) contexts. I am also referring to other evangelical traditions that share basic agreement on the gospel, soteriology, etc.

identify ourselves primarily as those who attend *his* church, or *the* church, and equate that with what it means to be right with God, then we are unwittingly opening the door to a subtle kind of works righteousness.

We may also seek to identify ourselves by our own particular practices. Whether it is the musical styles in our worship services, preaching so-called expository sermons instead of topical, reading certain books, homeschooling, fasting, drinking alcohol, teetotaling, or the clothing styles that function as uniforms in our churches (whether ties or flip-flops), we can elevate nearly anything to the place that Christ alone may occupy. It does not matter how good or proper or hip something may be; we will be tempted to seek our identity and justification in it.

The point of all this is that we love works and turning things into works. We love what we can see, point to, take pride in, and boast about. Works are, after all, so much easier than faith. Anyone can *do* things, but *believing*? That is a different story altogether. We are no different than the Galatians tinkering around with the law; we just have different ways of expressing it. The irony is that many of us spend a lot of time, paper, and ink speaking against works righteousness and the dangers associated with those who want to make works part of justification, all the while unaware that we like to do the same thing. It is just that our attempts at self-justification are more subtle, more orthodox, and more acceptable.

What we need is to see that everything, whether our ministries, traditions, associations, institutions, practices, or preferences, can be potential sidetracks from justification by faith; we can become slowly enslaved to good things that quietly lead us away from Christ. We need Paul's message to the Galatians: Christ has set us free from works (of the law and otherwise), and we are free to live according to faith and conscience (before the Lord), so why enslave ourselves and others "to the weak and worthless elementary principles of the world, whose slaves you want to be once more" (4:9)?

Falling from Grace

> You foolish Galatians! Who has bewitched you? Before your very
> eyes Jesus Christ was clearly portrayed as crucified. I would like
> to learn just one thing from you: Did you receive the Spirit by
> the works of the law, or by believing what you heard? Are you
> so foolish? After beginning by means of the Spirit, are you now
> trying to finish by means of the flesh? (3:1–3, NIV)

Paul directs the Galatians back to their own experience of
the gospel to show them the futility of self-justification. Seeking justification on any grounds other than Christ alone means
abandoning the gospel of Christ and trusting in ourselves—and
one does not have to turn consciously or verbally away from the
gospel to deny it practically. That is why Paul does not hold back
his language or tone when addressing the Galatians. He wants
them to understand the mortal danger of self-justification. Later
he tells them point blank about the consequence of seeking to
justify themselves by their works: "Look: I, Paul, say to you that
if you accept circumcision, Christ will be of no advantage to
you" (5:2). The reason that Christ will be of no value is because
adding circumcision means adding the entire law (v. 3), and Paul
has already made it clear that no one can be justified before God
by keeping the law (3:10–11). The law shows what God demands
and how far we fall short of meeting those demands in our fallen
condition. Therefore, any attempt to justify ourselves by law is "to
reject the reality about ourselves that the law reveals, to refuse
to submit to God in his contention with us."[4]

Now Paul weighs in with his most shocking statement in
a book filled with shocking statements: "You are severed from
Christ, you who would be justified by the law; you have fallen
away from grace" (5:4).[5] That is the capstone of the argument in
Galatians against those who want to add works to Christ. Both
the NIV and the ESV push the reader toward a slightly less drastic

4. Mark A. Seifrid, *Christ, Our Righteousness: Paul's Theology of Justification* (Downers Grove, IL: IVP, 2000), 149.
5. My translation.

interpretation by inserting the word *away,* with the result that Paul may seem to be speaking of what we might call *backsliding* rather than final condemnation. Inserting *away* gets at Paul's meaning, but we should not blunt the force of what he says. Paul's words here are no less stern than Jesus' words in John 15: "Every branch in me that does not bear fruit he [the Father] takes away" (v. 2). We may hear these words and immediately be distracted by discussions about whether we can lose our salvation, but that is not Paul's discussion at the moment.

This text is not about whether one may lose salvation generally but about the deadly result of self-justification. I do not think Paul is saying that anyone in Galatia has fallen from grace in an eternal sense at this point, but he is warning them of the *real* consequences of pursuing justification apart from or in addition to Christ. We must not take away from the power of Paul's words because of whatever presuppositions we may have about the security of the believer. The believer is secured by the Spirit through faith, but anyone who insists on justifying himself by works in the face of New Testament teaching like that found here in Galatians had better not presume to be justified in the sight of God.

Freedom in the Gospel

When Paul reminds the Galatians that Christ was crucified before their eyes (3:1), he does not mean that they were there at Calvary; he is talking about the proclamation of the gospel. He points them back to the truth of the gospel as the answer to the insanity of self-justification. We probably do not find the answer surprising. We *know* the answer. What is surprising is how often we speak, act, and live as though we do not even know the question, much less the answer. The good news is that the gospel is always the answer and the way out of the slavery of self-reliance. The gospel points us away from ourselves to God's free gift of righteousness. It is always the invitation to turn away from dead works that condemn us, that never satisfy us to the freedom found in Christ. The gospel is ever a call to repent and believe Christ, whose all-sufficient work justifies us from all the things from which the law could never justify us (Acts 13:39).

New Life in Christ

In Christ we have already died to the law, having been crucified in him who died under its curse for us (Gal. 2:19–20; 3:13). As a result of his death we have life—the very thing offered to Adam and through Moses but which we were never able to attain. The demand for works only produced death until One came to satisfy the will of God and bear the sins of Adam's children. Now life is ours through faith in union with Christ. That is why Paul locates the life of the believer in "Christ who lives in me" rather than in the old self (2:20). When Paul says, "It is no longer I who live," he is speaking of the old self in Adam (Rom. 6:6; Eph. 4:22; Col. 3:9), the old self who tried but failed to justify himself on the basis of works. That self was crucified on the cross of Christ, and the death sentence that hung over the old self was served on Christ, whose death and life become ours through faith.

Rather than the old self, condemned under the law, it is Christ who lives in the believer. Paul refers here to the presence of Christ in the believer through the Spirit in the new, end-time age in which we now live as a fulfillment of the promise of the new covenant. Galatians 2:20 should not be reduced to a phrase like "Jesus lives in my heart," for it encompasses the new covenant life in the Spirit. This is a prevalent theme in Galatians. In 3:2–3, where Paul speaks of receiving the Spirit and beginning by the Spirit, he is talking about the new covenant reality that has dawned in Christ and is proclaimed in the gospel. Similarly, in verse 12, where Paul says that the "law is not of faith," he is contrasting the time of the Mosaic law, which has passed, with the new era that has come through Christ in fulfillment of the promise to Abraham.[6] That is

6. This verse does not conflict with texts such as Romans 8:4 that speak of the law's being fulfilled by the believer through the Spirit but contrasts the era of the old covenant, which served the promise and pointed to Christ with the new covenant. Furthermore, Paul is not declaring that faith was nonexistent in the Sinai covenant.

173

why he can speak of the Mosaic covenant's being the time "before faith came" and the thing under which we were "imprisoned until the coming faith would be revealed" (v. 23). It played the role of guardian, "but now that faith has come," its role is over (v. 25). In the face of the overwhelming glory of the fulfillment of the new covenant, returning to righteousness through works is not only impossible but, in Paul's mind, inconceivable.

"Don't Choose Death, Receive Life"

Now that the new covenant has come, and with it justification by faith and new life in the Spirit, we might compare relying on works to wishing to be buried alive. Like other people, I have a fear of waking up only to find myself interred in a coffin, six feet underground. The slim to no chance of that happening does not stop an involuntary shudder from going up my spine if I think about it. Yet when we rest on our abilities, accomplishments, associations, and attainments, we are in effect voluntarily burying ourselves alive. We are members of the new covenant, enjoying the free gifts of justification, life, full acceptance by God, and a certain promise for the future, but against all better understanding and wisdom we unwittingly build tombs made of works.

All of this may sound somewhat bleak and pessimistic, but with Paul we must deal openly and unequivocally with all attempts at self-justification, and also with Paul we have to hold out the reality of the grace of God in Christ to ourselves and others. That is why, I think, that Galatians is sprinkled throughout with the message of the gospel. Paul does not just lambaste the Galatians and at the end ask them to come forward and repent; he reinforces the message of the gospel in every chapter. Paul is hopeful that the Galatians will make a full recovery from the works sickness infecting them. As he did with Peter in Antioch, he reminds the Galatians of who they really are in Christ as evidenced by their own experience of the gospel.[7] They began with the unadulter-

7. See 3:1–5, 26–28; 4:1–10, 12–15; 5:1, 5–7, 13, 18–23, 25.

ated gospel, faith, and the Spirit, and that was all they needed, and all they need now.

Near the end of the letter, Paul makes a final contrast with seeking righteousness by works—the promise of life held out by the law that was unattainable through the law belongs now to the believer through the certain hope of a final declaration of righteousness: "For through the Spirit, by faith, we ourselves eagerly wait for the hope of righteousness" (5:5). The righteousness that Paul speaks of here is the future hope of the believer.[8] What they are now in Christ will be openly declared in the future. On the last day God will declare them unequivocally and forever righteous before him apart from works. In light of the coming day, all attempts at self-justification should begin to fade from view. The eschatological hope of the gospel is part of Paul's remedy to works righteousness.

Faith Working through Love

Virtually anything, even what we do *not* do, can become something in which we place our trust. Paul overturns both the tendency to rely on works and the misplaced self-satisfaction that may arise from *not* doing works: "For in Christ Jesus neither circumcision nor uncircumcision counts for anything, but only faith working through love" (5:6). This verse underpins verse 5 by showing that nothing other than Spirit-driven faith in Christ counts before God and provides the hope for the coming declaration of righteousness at the end time. Paul's reminder that circumcision counts for nothing in terms of righteousness before God is in keeping with his emphasis in the majority of the letter, but he is also quick to fend off any sort of self-assurance that may arise from *avoiding* the lure of works.

It is not difficult to imagine what Paul speaks against. Someone in Galatia might think, "Unlike *those* people who put their

---

8. For a clear discussion of this fairly difficult verse, see Thomas R. Schreiner, *Galatians*, Exegetical Commentary on the New Testament (Grand Rapids: Zondervan, 2010), 313–14.

trust in works, I know that works can never justify, and there is no way that I will ever submit to circumcision; my understanding of the truth of the gospel is clearly superior to their law-based way of life." It is like the way we often decry works righteousness while taking pride in our freedom from the legalism so prevalent in *other* Christians. So we might think, *"Those* Christians with their rules, their 'do this' and 'don't do that,' have never understood the gospel; we, however, have the true gospel and are free from such legalistic nonsense." We quickly forget that whatever we have or understand is a gift from God, and it is the height of arrogance to act as though we conjured up anything good in ourselves apart from God's grace (1 Cor. 4:7). It is right to deny legalism and to embrace the freedom of the gospel, but as soon as our so-called freedom becomes yet another badge to represent our own accomplishments and identity, we may as well be keeping every rule in the book and relying on our works. Paul reminds them, and us, that as a ground for God's declaration that we are justified in his sight, uncircumcision is as useless as circumcision. What counts is faith that expresses itself in love for others.

Once more we see the outward trajectory of justification. Just as the biblical doctrine of justification by faith points us away from ourselves to God, so too it directs us away from ourselves to others. For the justified, life is not about us but about others. It is loving God and loving neighbor all over again. Paul is not saying that our actions, even love that flows from faith, are a basis for our justification. Such a conclusion can hardly be supported from reading Galatians. However, as we saw in the last chapter, Paul, like James, does not envision faith as a vacuum but as something that is filled with and shows itself through works.[9] It is not *faith-works*, or *faith/works*, but faith that flows out into the "good works, which God prepared beforehand, that we should walk in them" (Eph. 2:10). It is the new life in the Spirit to which Paul directs the attention of the Galatians as another part of the remedy to works righteousness. Ridderbos puts the idea of Galatians 6:5 like this:

9. "Faith, of course, is not a nullity. It is living and active and powerful. It expresses itself in love." Schreiner, *Galatians*, 317.

The thought contains the two truths that love is fruitful (cf. James 2:22) and that the energy of the works which love produces is quite different from the "works" of the law. This energy is a working of faith which has its principle and its source in the life-giving power of the Spirit. In accordance with the promise and in communion with Christ's death and resurrection it brings into manifestation also the new life of believers.[10]

The "new life" comes up again later in Galatians in a similar verse: "For neither circumcision counts for anything, nor uncircumcision, but a new creation" (6:15). The "new creation" parallels "faith working through love" in 5:6 and so links the life of faith to the work of God through the Spirit. Believers are freed from slavery to deadly works to a life led by the Spirit, lived in the Spirit, and bearing the Spirit's fruit, the first of which is love (5:18, 22–25).

Fulfilling Christ's Law

The other-centered remedy to works righteousness is summed up in 6:2: "Bear one another's burdens, and so fulfill the law of Christ." The "law of Christ" is highly debated, but the best interpretive key is found in the context. In 5:14 Paul says that "the whole law is fulfilled in one word: 'You shall love your neighbor as yourself.'" By quoting Leviticus 19:18, Paul shows the Galatians that as inheritors of the new covenant, they are now in the position to pursue the intent of the law from the right starting place. Rather than working toward a life that could never be attained through law ("the one who does them shall live by them"—3:12, quoting Lev. 18:5), the believer, now justified by faith in Christ, is free to serve and live for others. That is the freedom of the gospel—freedom to stop living for self and instead to live as God intended and as God enables through the Spirit.

The law of Christ is best understood in terms of Christ's being the appointed end and fulfillment of the law (3:13–14, 24–25; cf. Rom. 10:4; Matt. 5:17), and as a result believers are empowered to

10. Herman N. Ridderbos, *The Epistle of Paul to the Churches of Galatia* (Grand Rapids: Eerdmans, 1953), 191.

fulfill the other-focused intent of the great commands to love God and love neighbor—the essence of the law. So the law of Christ is not the new covenant version of the Mosaic law in which the hundreds of commands can now be kept through the Spirit; it is the manifestation and fulfillment of the law of love (Lev. 19:18) in the life of the believer. Such a law can only be pursued through the eschatological gift of the Spirit and the new heart embroidered with the law, as promised in Jeremiah 33 and Ezekiel 36.

Radical Freedom

The word *remedy* appears several times in the preceding paragraphs. I use this word because Paul offers his admonishments, warnings, and reminders as the means by which the Galatians will turn from themselves to God and others. Paul is confident that the Galatians, upon reading his letter, will accept what he has to say and leave their dalliances with self-justification behind: "I have confidence in the Lord that you will take no other view" (5:10). Self-justification is the disease, and the gospel—justification through faith in Christ alone—and the new life offered through the Spirit are the cure. As strange as it may sound, the life of the justified, a life in which God and neighbor take center stage and self-centeredness is killed, is a life of freedom.

We have such small and often secular ideas of freedom that envision it as what we want, how we want it, and when we want it. Our petty notions of freedom are typically based only on what we are allowed to partake in, enjoy, and consume, and we can miss the true freedom that we have as believers justified in Christ. Here is how radical our freedom really is: we are so free that we can voluntarily put aside our own personal freedoms and desires for the sake of others. It may sound like a contradiction to some people, but Christian freedom is freedom to live for something besides our own interests, appetites, and ambitions. In fact, when we discover this truth, we will find that the real and satisfying fulfillment of our desires is in God and neighbor rather than in ourselves. This is the end result of justification—we are made right with God so that we can become the true children of the true Adam and, like him, give ourselves to God and to those around us. It is a radically other-centered life, and it is exactly how true human life is envisioned in the Bible.

Free to Obey

We often do not know exactly what to do with commands in the New Testament. One problem is that we do not distinguish between works as a starting point and works, or obedience, as a result of faith. The difference is immeasurable. There are commands all over the New Testament, including Galatians. Not only is there the great command to love your neighbor, but Paul also commands us to avoid conceit, provocation, and envy (5:26); he commands those who are spiritual to restore those caught in sin (6:1); everyone is to bear one another's burdens (v. 2); each is to test his own works (v. 4); the one taught the word must share the word with others (v. 6); we are not to become tired of doing good (v. 9); and, we are to do good to everyone (v. 10). Clearly, Paul envisions obedience to these commands to be via empowerment by the Spirit, but we should not look at these commands as any less real than other commands in the Bible. We should begin thinking about New Testament obedience as Luther does: "Faith does not ask whether there are good works to do, but before the question arises, it has already done them, and is always doing them."[11] We should not take that to mean that just saying "I believe" is the New Testament way of obedience but that when we begin with faith, commands are not burdensome or overwhelming; they are the words of the living God to his people in order to reveal his will for us and for which he gives us his Spirit for empowerment. Does this mean that we will perfectly obey, or that a works-righteousness mentality cannot creep in? It never means either of those things for the present time. What it means is that those who truly grasp their justification, are in a right standing

11. Preface to *Romans*.

before God, are forgiven of their sins, and have Christ as their righteousness are released to pursue justice and righteousness in obedience to their covenant God. Through the Spirit and by God's grace we can reimage obedience as flowing from faith and so be set free from "Jesus *and* . . . ."

Justification Freedom in South Asia

A few years ago I encountered a real-life illustration of the freedom that justification brings, and it brought that truth home as well as anything that I have experienced. One summer, while teaching in South Asia, I spent several days with Muslim-background believers. Many of these brothers were former leaders in mosques or their villages and towns. Each day two men who were clearly close friends sat in the front, asking questions, helping with translation, and eagerly taking part in discussions. Both men were former imams (leaders in a mosque, something like a pastor/preacher), both well educated, knowledgeable in the Scriptures, and as knowledgeable in the Koran as anyone I have met. There was one obvious difference between them. One man wore khaki pants and a collared shirt every day while the other wore traditional dress: long white shirt, white pants, and a white skull cap. We spent a great deal of time one day talking about Abraham and justification, moving from the Old Testament to the New Testament—a large portion of the time was spent working through what later became the basic content of this book. Near the end of our time together, I finally asked them why they dressed differently. The one in the khaki pants answered first: "For me, I cannot wear the traditional clothes because that is what I wore before knowing Christ. I only associate those clothes with who I was. When I share the gospel, I want to tell people what I am now." The other answered in this way: "This is what I have always worn. These clothes are comfortable, not hot and tight like those [pointing and smiling at his khaki-clad friend]. Dressing this way means nothing to me. Also when I dress this way, I can go into mosques and into villages to share the gospel without making an obstacle of what I wear." I then asked the man in khakis, "Should he stop wearing those clothes?" He answered, "He is free to dress as he likes, as I am. What matters is that we are true to Christ." Much to everyone's surprise, I shouted, "Yes! That's it!" They both understood that their style of dress means nothing (khakis are nothing and kurta pajamas are nothing); it is a matter of conscience and mission as faith works its way in love. Even though both had solid convictions for dressing in particular ways, neither man understood his clothing as what identifies or distinguishes one from the other. This is the kind of freedom that justification brings: freedom from the burden of adding to or taking from what God gives us in Christ.

Conclusion:
The Biblical, Central,
and Practical Doctrine
of Justification

IT IS TIME to put things together and further apply them to our hearts.

- A Biblical Doctrine: Summing Up the Narrative of Justification
- A Core Doctrine
- A Doctrine to Proclaim
- Keeping Justification in Perspective

A Biblical Doctrine: Summing Up the Narrative of Justification

Justification is God's verdict that in Christ and on the basis of Christ's life, death, and resurrection our sins are forgiven and we are counted as those who are perfectly obedient in his sight. In other words, God declares us to be righteous.

When we think of justification, we may think only of Paul, but with Paul (Rom. 4:1–8) we need to remember that the doctrine did not originate with him. A right understanding of justification cannot focus only on Romans or Galatians (or any other New Testament text) but must be grounded in the Bible from Eden onward. The goal of the covenantal relationship between Adam and God was eternal life, but that goal was seemingly cut short by Adam's disobedience. As a result, sin and death flowed into the world, and Adam's children come into the world under God's wrath. The curse from Adam's disobedience hangs over the human race. The solution hinted at in Genesis 3:15, the woman's seed defeating the seed of the serpent, begins to unfold in Shem's genealogy, which leads to Abraham, who is justified by faith in the God who promises to bless the world (Gen. 12:3; 26:4). It is at this point that faith and righteousness are bound explicitly together in the Bible. God declares Abraham to be righteous by faith and guarantees his covenant with Abraham and his children, but the true children of Abraham, those who inherit the promise, will be marked as those who do justice and righteousness (18:17–19).

With the establishment of the Mosaic law comes a clear word from God regarding what he intends and expects from his people. Righteousness will be theirs if they obey everything that God says (Deut. 6:25), but they are told what it is going to take to fulfill the righteous requirement of the law—a new heart (10:16). Ultimately, God himself will provide the new heart needed to stand before him (30:6). Israel's experience with the law clearly shows that no one will be right with God on the basis of the works required by the law. Yet the covenantal promise to Abraham pulsates through the Scripture, awaiting fulfillment. The prophets announce a coming day when God will write his law on the hearts of his people and pour out his Spirit on them so that they will be his people and he their God (Jer. 31:31–34; Ezek. 36:24–27). God will accomplish this through his obedient servant, who will justify God's people by bearing their grief, sorrow, and sin (Isa. 53).

The fulfillment of the promise to Abraham and the fulfillment of the law come to a climax in Christ, who dies under the curse of the law in order to bring about the blessing promised to Abraham (Gal. 3:14). In Christ, God reveals his righteousness in judging sin on the cross to save all who put their faith in Jesus. By faith, sinners are legally and forever declared by God to be in the right, having the perfect righteousness of Christ counted to them (Rom. 4:1–8; 2 Cor. 5:21). Christ attained that righteousness through his obedience as the second Adam (Rom. 5:18–19), and through him we are justified and inherit the goal for which God created the world—eternal life in Christ.

A Core Doctrine

These days it is common to hear people point out that justification features prominently only in letters that address Jew-Gentile relations in regard to questions concerning the law. Rather than lying at the core of Paul's theology, justification is largely reserved for contexts marked by controversy, as in Galatians. Likewise, when Paul wants to make it clear that Jews and Gentiles stand on the same ground before God, as in Romans, justification plays a major role in his discussion. From this perspective, the doctrine is viewed as largely polemical (against another view) rather than central. There is much to be gained from recognizing the Jew-Gentile tension in the early church as partly motivating the teaching on justification found in the New Testament. For one, it helps us to read letters like Romans and Galatians in their context and not simply as abstracted theological essays. But overemphasizing the claim that Paul's doctrine of justification was reserved primarily for tensions between Jewish and Gentile believers suffers from the "throwing-the-baby-out-with-the-bathwater" syndrome.

Take, for example, Paul's letter to Titus. The letter is written to a young church in Crete, and Paul ends the letter with an overview of salvation in Christ.

> But when the goodness and loving kindness of God our Savior appeared, he saved us, not because of works done by us in righteousness, but according to his own mercy, by the washing of regeneration and renewal of the Holy Spirit, whom he poured out on us richly through Jesus Christ our Savior, so that being justified by his grace we might become heirs according to the hope of eternal life. (Titus 3:4–7)

The passage is relatively short, yet thorough. John Stott sums up verses 3–8 as "the ingredients of salvation," which include the *need*, *source*, *ground*, *means*, *goal*, and *evidence* of salvation.[1] Justification, in Stott's summary, is included in the *goal* of salvation.[2] Our justification is tied directly to the ultimate goal of life—embedded in creation since Eden. This is similar to the emphasis found in Romans 4:25, where Jesus' resurrection results in our justification, and Romans 5:19, where Jesus' obedience leads to justification and life. The point is that in Titus, Paul is not dealing specifically with Jew-Gentile or law issues but is presenting his fundamental doctrine of salvation, with justification, among other things, at the core.

Justification in Titus is not just a link in a chain, nor is it simply tied to controversy, but is connected directly to the phrase "he saved us." The "so that" in verse 7 links "justified" back to "saved" in verse 5. We were saved on the basis of God's mercy (v. 5) through the cleansing of the Holy Spirit (vv. 5–6) so that we who are judged to be righteous in the sight of God now may have life. Justification is bound to God's entire work of salvation because it is only through the declaration of righteousness that we attain God's intended goal for us. If the aim of salvation is life (the original purpose in creation), then the only way for *sinners* to have life is first to be justified. As for the work of the Spirit, note that it is not a case of "either/or" but "both/and." Those who inherit eternal life "are those both transformed by God's Spirit . . . and declared righteous by God's grace."[3]

It is also worth noting that justification comes up in Titus in the midst of the same concepts and ideas found in the other justification texts. In Titus 3:5, Paul asserts that salvation is not based on "works done by us in righteousness," an idea echoed in other justification texts such as Galatians 2:16, Philippians 3:9, and Romans 3:20. On the other end of Paul's salvation outline, he tells

1. John R. W. Stott, *Guard the Truth: The Message of 1 Timothy and Titus* (Downers Grove: IVP, 1996), 200–208. Emphasis original.

2. That is not to say that our justification is pushed completely into the future. Christians are justified by faith now, but that verdict from God will be openly declared in the future.

3. George Knight, *Commentary on the Pastoral Epistles*, New International Greek Testament Commentary (Grand Rapids, Eerdmans, 1992), 346.

Titus to "insist on these things, so that those who have believed in God may be careful to devote themselves to good works" (3:8). The idea of good works flowing from justification basically makes up the latter part of Galatians, and as seen earlier, James insists that a true declaration of righteousness from God *must* flow out into obedience. As for Romans, the Jew-Gentile question is prominent, but the letter is also a kind of theological introduction to a group of people who did not yet know Paul face to face.

Justification is not just for controversy—whether first- or twenty-first-century controversy—but is vital to the church in every era and in every circumstance. We must always turn our attention, and the attention of those in the pews, classrooms, mission fields, workplaces, coffee shops, and houses across the street, to what it means— and what it has taken—for people to be right with God. If we follow Paul, we will focus on justification as a core doctrine of the faith.

A Doctrine to Proclaim

The primary arena for justification is proclamation. In other words, justification is for the pulpit and pew. While books and conferences will reach certain audiences, it is people who live and work day to day who need most to hear the message of justification by faith in Christ apart from works. If we only *talk* about justification with a particular group of interested people who follow the debates, then our doctrine of justification is of limited use. Justification is not an academic exercise— a quick scan of Galatians should be enough to prove that. After all, anything less than justification by faith alone amounts to a false gospel, and that is hardly an academic point.

Preaching to Hearts, Not Just Heads

A sermon on justification should not be aimed primarily at dispensing information but at hearts and lives enslaved to the idea that God's acceptance or rejection of them is ultimately

187

based on what they do and what they have accomplished—whether good or bad. It is difficult to *believe* that we are "justified by his grace as a gift." It is not difficult to agree with the idea or affirm it in theory, but it is quite another thing to hold to it practically and to rest in it. The inclination that Adam had to go his own way when tempted, and the attempt by the people at Shinar to build a tower and establish their own way apart from God, have done anything but fade over the millennia. Such attitudes are not just "out there" in the world but more seriously are inside churches. Pews are filled with people who practically believe that God will accept them because they never committed so-called serious sins. Likewise, there are people who may make much of salvation through faith alone in Christ alone, but when they go home, out of the public eye, there is no evidence or influence of God's justifying grace in their lives. Singing "And Can It Be?" rouses their sense of orthodoxy and gives a tingle down the spine, but the truth in the lyrics never touches the heart.

On the other hand, many people suffer not from resting in their own accomplishments but from the fear that God will never accept them because of overwhelming guilt and shame for sin. They know God is righteous, and it terrifies them. They sing "And Can it Be?" and think, "No, it can't, not for me." They affirm that a right standing before God is by faith alone, but they cannot shake the idea that somehow their sin is more powerful than God's justifying word. Crushed by sin, they live in a prison of doubt, dread, and fear. Rather than believe what God says, they believe Satan's accusations and the confused ramblings running through their minds. They are enslaved to themselves every bit as much as the self-righteous. They need again, like the young C. H. Spurgeon, to hear "Look unto me, and be ye saved" (Isa. 45:22), and hear that the God who calls them "speaks the truth" about them, that when he declares them to be justified, he is proclaiming "what is right" (v. 19). Only by grasping God's justifying word can they turn to the accuser and say to the voices in their heads, "Yes, I am an ungodly sinner, but Christ lived, died, and rose for me, and now I am washed, sanctified, and justified in him—that is what God says, and he always speaks the truth." It takes faith to believe in justification by faith, and it takes faithful pastors, teachers, and friends to point doubt and fear-laden brothers and sisters to Christ.

Whether duped by works or defeated by guilt, the cure, to be reapplied continually, is the message that the only thing needed to make us right with God is Jesus' blood and righteousness. In some seasons we need to hear that trusting in works means rejecting and cutting ourselves off from Christ (Gal. 5:4). At other times we need to grasp, even if only by a thread, that it is precisely the ungodly that God justifies apart from works (Rom. 4:4). As legalists and antinomians, we need a constant reminder that the Lord is our righteousness (Jer. 23:6; 33:16), that nothing can be added or taken away from him.

Motivating Good Works

Someone might read the previous comments and say, "You are just giving everyone license to do whatever they please because, at the end of the day, how they live does not matter since they have the righteousness of Christ." I reply that what preaching and teaching this view of justification *can* lead to and what it *should* lead to are not the same thing. Rightly understood and taught in its biblical entirety, justification by faith alone should lead to a healthy motivation to live the life of the justified. That kind of life is free from a performance mentality and sees works and obedience as flowing from the freedom found in God's gift of righteousness and flowing back to him in thanksgiving and faithfulness. God does not only designate righteousness; he also creates what he declares. Those justified by faith, counted righteous through Christ's righteousness, are a "new creation" (2 Cor. 5:17), and as such they possess the Spirit-filled heart that God promised in Jeremiah 31 and Ezekiel 36. God's justifying verdict in Christ creates children of Abraham who do the justice and righteousness fitting the inheritors of the promise.

No one can deny that preaching justification by faith alone *can* lead to lawlessness—Paul foresaw this very possibility in Romans 6. We cannot hold back on justification just because some people may mishear and misuse the Scripture. Nevertheless, in some cases it is the result of an error in preaching and teaching, of failing to grasp justification by faith alone in connection with the larger biblical doctrine of salvation. Rightly understood, justification by faith alone is the key to understanding Christian obedience because it reorients us away from ourselves to God and neighbor.

When Christians obey, they have a foretaste of that coming day when everything down to the pots and pans will be stamped "Holy to the LORD" (Zech. 14:20). Obedience does not always bring our best life now, but it does mean taking part now in the best life still to come when we stand before God justified in the second Adam. Thomas Kelly put it like this:

> Then we shall be where we would be;
>   then we shall be what we should be;
> things which are not now, nor could be,
>   then shall be our own.[4]

Keeping Justification in Perspective

No one is saved by believing in justification. No one is forgiven, cleansed, sanctified, or glorified by believing in justification. No one, for that matter, is justified by believing in justification. We are saved—forgiven, justified, sanctified, and glorified—by faith in Christ alone. Writing in the midst of controversy over justification, the Scottish pastor Robert Traill reflects on what to tell a man who is convicted of his sins and seeking salvation. The answer is well known and often repeated: "Believe in the Lord Jesus Christ, and you will be saved, you and your household" (Acts 16:30–31). If the man continues to ask "What he is to believe?," Traill advises this response:

4. From the hymn "Praise the Savior Ye Who Know Him."

Tell him that he is not called to believe that he is in Christ; that his sins are pardoned, and he is a justified man; but that he is to believe God's record concerning Christ (1 John 5:10–12), and this record is that God gives (that is, offers) to us eternal life in his Son Jesus Christ, and that all that with the heart believe this report, and rest their souls on these glad tidings, shall be saved (Rom. 10:9–11). And thus he is to believe that he may be justified. (Gal. 2:16)[5]

It is easy to forget that justification by itself is not the gospel. We do not offer people justification—we point them to Christ so that by faith they might be justified and saved.

When we proclaim the gospel, we announce that God has opened the way to himself through Christ and that all who lay hold of Christ by faith are fully acceptable and pleasing to God. We announce that the endless cycle of guilt-ridden despair that comes from chasing the happiness, contentment, and satisfaction that Adam's children have craved since that dark day in Eden has ended, that we may now stand before God without guilt, perfectly righteous in his sight. Christ, the second and last Adam, died and rose just as the Scriptures say, and all who believe in him have eternal life. All this is ours through God's gift of righteousness in Christ.

5. Robert Traill, *Justification Vindicated*, Puritan Paperbacks (Edinburgh: Carlisle, 2002), 29.

Questions for Study and Reflection

Introduction—"Look unto Me, and Be Ye Saved"

1. What comes to mind when you hear the word *justification*?
2. Why is the idea of turning from ourselves to God important in the doctrine of justification?
3. Why is it vital to stress that justification is first about Christ?

Chapter 1—The Legacy of Adam

1. Why is it important to stress that we are created and dependent on God? Why is this basic biblical truth such a difficult idea for us in the twenty-first century?

2. Explain what it means to say that there is one goal for creation, including human beings, from the beginning.

3. What are some reasons for supporting the idea that there was a covenant in the garden of Eden? What reasons might someone have to say there was no covenant in Eden?

4. What do we learn about obedience and faith from the story of Adam? How does that affect our reading of the rest of the Bible and the way in which we think about justification?

Chapter 2—The Obedient Second and Last Adam

1. How has Adam's sin affected all of us? Does God punish us for Adam's sin?

2. In what ways can we compare Adam and Christ? In what ways can we contrast them?

3. Why is it necessary to say that Christ's obedience was both active and passive? What texts in the Bible support that idea?

4. What does Paul mean in Romans 5:19 when he says that many will be "made" righteous? What does "made" mean in that context?

Chapter 3—Not By Sight: Abraham and the Righteousness of Faith

1. What are some of the events in Genesis 3–11 that leave the reader with little doubt about the inability of people to make themselves right with God?

2. The word *believed* first appears in the Bible in Genesis 15:6. Discuss why it is significant that the word appears there for the first time. Was that the first time that anyone had faith in God?

3. What does it mean for God to "reckon" Abraham's faith as righteousness?

4. The covenant in Genesis 15 is often referred to as unconditional. Discuss what that means, and also discuss ways in which the word *unconditional* might be misunderstood. How does Genesis 18:17–19 affect the way we think about the covenant with Abraham?

5. How does the story of Abraham set the scene for how we understand righteousness and justification in the rest of the Bible?

Chapter 4—Abraham: Our Father according to the Faith

1. Explain how imputation is connected to the larger doctrine of justification.

2. What separates biblical faith from the way faith is often spoken of in our society?

3. Why is it vital to speak of faith as a means of justification?

4. Why does the imputation language in Romans 4 imply both forgiveness and a positive counting of righteousness?

5. Discuss the second quotation of Genesis 15:6 in Romans 4, found in verse 22. Why does Paul repeat the quote?

Chapter 5—The Law: Things by Which You Cannot Be Justified

1. It is sometimes said that it would be unfair for God to give a law that he knew people could not keep. Do you believe that God knew Israel could not keep the law? If so, how would you explain to people that it was not unfair of God to do so?

2. How was the giving of the law an act of grace on God's part?

3. Name some ways that the Mosaic covenant is both like and unlike the covenant with Abraham.

4. What did God teach the nation of Israel through the Mosaic law? How and what does he teach us through reading the narrative of Israel's history?

5. What are the main Old Testament texts that point forward to God's providing the hearts needed to fulfill his commands? Can you think of other texts beyond the ones mentioned in this book?

Chapter 6—God's Righteousness and Ours

1. How would you respond if someone asked, "What does 'the righteousness of God' mean?" Can you give some Bible texts with your answer?

2. What is works righteousness? Did the law teach works righteousness?

3. According to Paul in Romans 10:3–4, what was wrong with the way in which many Jews pursued the law?

4. What is the righteousness that Paul counts on in Philippians 3:9? How is that different from his righteousness prior to knowing Christ?

5. Why is the doctrine of union with Christ so important for the doctrine of justification? How does it provide comfort and assurance?

Chapter 7—Faith Works: The Life of the Justified

1. What kind of faith is James denying in James 2:14–26?

2. How many connections can you think of between James's teaching in chapter 2 of his letter and the teaching of Jesus in the Gospels?

3. Discuss the perspectives of James and Paul on the life and actions of Abraham.

4. How is justification connected to the past, present, and future?

5. Explain in the simplest terms possible what it means to say, "We are justified by faith alone, but justifying faith is never alone."

Chapter 8—Freedom: Justification Applied

1. What were the two main problems with the attempts by the Judaizers to add the law to faith in Christ?

2. List some ways in which you tend to live by what is referred to in this chapter as "Jesus *and* . . . ."

3. What did Paul mean when he said that the Galatians had "fallen from grace" (Gal. 5:4)?

4. Discuss ways in which the biblical doctrine of justification brings freedom to the Christian.

5. What does justification restore us to do in terms of living as the true people of God?

Conclusion—The Biblical, Central, and Practical Doctrine of Justification

1. Why is justification a core doctrine of the Christian faith?

2. What correction does the doctrine of justification offer to the self-righteous—even the self-righteous who find their assurance in affirming orthodox creeds and confessions?

3. How does the right application of justification offer comfort to those in despair over sin and hopelessness?

4. How would you tell an unbeliever with no Bible or church background about the doctrine of justification? What texts would you share? What essential ideas would you share with them?

5. In what ways can you apply the doctrine of justification to your own life?

Select Resources on Justification

Bird, Michael. *Introducing Paul: The Man, His Mission and His Message*. Downers Grove: IVP, 2008.

Buchanan, James. *The Doctrine of Justification: An Outline of Its History in the Church and of Its Exposition from Scripture*. Edinburgh: T. & T. Clark, 1867. Reprint. Grand Rapids, Baker, 1955. For a long while this book was held by many to be one of the primary sources for and expositions of a Reformed view of justification.

Calvin, John. *Institutes of the Christian Religion*. 2 vols. Translated by Ford Lewis Battles. Edited by John T. McNeill. Library of Christian Classics, vols. 20–21. Philadelphia: Westminster, 1960. See especially Book 3, chapters 11–19.

Clark, R. Scott, ed. *Covenant, Justification, and Pastoral Ministry: Essays by the Faculty of Westminster Seminary California*. Phillipsburg, NJ: P&R Publishing, 2007. Many excellent essays on justification and covenantal issues.

Fesko, J. V. *Justification: Understanding the Classic Reformed Doctrine*. Phillipsburg, NJ: P&R Publishing, 2008. Like Buchanan in his generation, Fesko offers a thorough presentation of the Reformed doctrine for readers today.

Gaffin, Richard B. *Resurrection and Redemption: A Study in Paul's Soteriology*. 2nd ed. Phillipsburg, NJ: Presbyterian and Reformed, 1987.

Luther, Martin. *Martin Luther's Basic Theological Writings*. Edited by Timothy F. Lull. Minneapolis: Fortress, 1989. This is the best one-volume collection of Luther's works. For those who want to read Luther for themselves and want a collection of some of Luther's most important works in one place (instead of the excellent but massive *Works*), this is the book to get. See especially the following: *Heidelberg*

Disputation; "Concerning the Letter and the Spirit"; *Preface to the New Testament*; *Preface to the Old Testament*; *How Christians Should Regard Moses* (1525); *Two Kinds of Righteousness* (the most important work in this book for understanding Luther's view of God's righteousness); *The Freedom of the Christian* (1520).

Murray, John. *Redemption Accomplished and Applied*. Grand Rapids: Eerdmans, 1955.

Owen, John. *The Works of John Owen*. Edited by William H. Gold. Vol. 5, *Faith and Its Evidences*. Carlisle, PA: Banner of Truth, 1965. This work could easily fit in the list below. Readers would be well served to read Fesko before beginning Owen.

Piper, John. *Counted Righteous in Christ*: *Should We Abandon the Imputed Righteousness of Christ?* Wheaton: Crossway, 2002. Piper responds to arguments against a traditional view of imputation. This book is exegetical and pastoral.

Schreiner, Thomas R. *Paul, Apostle of God's Glory in Christ: A Pauline Theology*. Downers Grove: InterVarsity, 2001.

Vos, Geerhardus. *Biblical Theology: Old and New Testaments*. Grand Rapids: Eerdmans, 1948.

_____. *The Pauline Eschatology*. Princeton: Princeton University Press, 1930. Reprint. Phillipsburg, NJ: P&R Publishing, 1994.

Witsius, Herman. *The Economy of the Covenants Between God and Man*. Translated by William Crookshank. London: R. Baynes, 1822. Reprint. Den Dulk Christian Foundation: Kingsburg, CA, 1990. A seminal presentation of historical covenant theology. Some of Witsius's interpretation of various texts is strained in service of his covenantal framework, but that does not take away from the importance and impact of this work.

Resources for Further Study

THE FOLLOWING RESOURCES are for readers who want to do further study on justification or explore some of the issues related to the New Perspective on Paul and the modern debates on justification.

Bird, Michael F. *Saving Righteousness of God: Studies in Paul, Justification, and the New Perspective*. PBM. Milton Keynes: Paternoster, 2007.

Das, A. Andrew. *Paul, the Law, and the Covenant*. Peabody: Hendrickson, 2001.

Gathercole, Simon J. *Where Is Boasting? Early Jewish Soteriology and Paul's Response in Romans 1–5*. Grand Rapids: Eerdmans, 2002.

Seifrid, Mark A. *Christ Our Righteousness: Paul's Theology of Justification*. Downers Grove: InterVarsity, 2001.

Waters, Guy Prentiss. *Justification and the New Perspectives on Paul: A Review and Response*. Phillipsburg, NJ: P&R Publishing, 2004.

Westerholm, Steven. *Perspectives Old and New on Paul: The "Lutheran Paul" and His Critics*. Grand Rapids: Eerdmans, 2004.

Wright, N. T. *What Saint Paul Really Said: Was Saul of Tarsus the Real Founder of Christianity?* Grand Rapids: Eerdmans, 1997. Although not as thorough as Wright's more recent book on justification (see below), much of what he has to say in this book is foundational for his view.

The best-known modern debate on justification took place between John Piper and N. T. Wright. The debate can be followed in these two books:

Piper, John. *The Future of Justification: A Response to N. T. Wright*. Wheaton: Crossway, 2007.

Wright, N. T. *Justification: God's Plan & Paul's Vision*. Downers Grove: IVP, 2009.

Index of Scripture

3:8–10—9n4
3:9—133–34, 186, 196

Colossians
1:14—139
3:9—173
4:1—49

1 Thessalonians
4:14—134

1 Timothy
3:16—46

2 Timothy
3:16—147
4:8—49

Titus
1:5—47n28
1:8—49
3:3—27
3:3–8—185
3:4–7—124, 185
3:5—186
3:5–6—124, 186
3:7—27, 124, 186
3:8—187

Hebrews
5:1—47n28
8:10—21n8
8:13—22
9:15—22
10:4—99
11:1—89n19, 154
11:4—52
11:8—58
11:31—154
12:24—22

James
1:3—143
1:5—143

1:12—143
1:17–18—143
1:18—146
1:22—143
1:23–24—143
1:25—146
1:26—143
1:27—144
2—161, 196
2:1—145
2:6—146
2:8—144, 146
2:4—145
2:9—145
2:10—101, 146
2:10–11—146
2:12—146
2:14—147
2:14–26—142, 196
2:15–16—148
2:17—148
2:18—149
2:18–23—148
2:19—149
2:20—150
2:21—150–51
2:22—153, 177
2:23—153
2:24—141, 154
2:25—154

1 Peter
1:7—158

2 Peter
1:8—48n29

1 John
5:10–12—191

Revelation
9:1—150
20:1—150
21:3—21n8

Index of Subjects and Names